STEP UP
YOUR SCRAPBOOKING

Pages You Can Create with 2, 3, 4 and More Supplies

by Lisa Brown Caveney

Editor-in-Chief	TRACY WHITE
Founding Editor	LISA BEARNSON
Special Projects Editor	LESLIE MILLER
Senior Editor, Special Projects	VANESSA HOY
Senior Writer	RACHEL THOMAE
Associate Writer	LORI FAIRBANKS
Assistant Writer	HEATHER JONES
Assistant Editor	BRITNEY MELLEN
Copy Editor	KIM SANDOVAL
Editorial Assistants	JOANNIE MCBRIDE, FRED BREWER
Art Director	BRIAN TIPPETTS
Senior Designer	ERIN BAYLESS
Photographers	SKYLAR NIELSEN, GAIGE REDD
Co-Founder	DON LAMBSON

PRIMEDIA
Consumer Magazine & Internet Group

PRIMEDIA, INC.

Chairman	DEAN NELSON
President and CEO	KELLY CONLIN
Vice-Chairman	BEVERLY C. CHELL
VP, Group Publisher	DAVID O'NEIL
Circulation Marketing Directors	DENA SPAR, JANICE MARTIN
Promotions Director	DANA SMITH

PRIMEDIA OUTDOOR RECREATION & ENTHUSIAST GROUP

President	SCOTT WAGNER
Group CFO	HENRY DONAHUE
VP, Marketing / Internet Operations	DAVE EVANS

CONSUMER MARKETING, PRIMEDIA ENTHUSIAST MEDIA

VP, Single Copy Marketing	RICH BARON
VP & CFO, Consumer Marketing	JENNIFER PRATHER
VP, Retail Analysis / Development	DOUG JENSEN
VP, Wholesale / Retail	STEFAN KAISER
VP, Consumer Marketing Operations	ELIZABETH MOSS

CONSUMER MARKETING, ENTHUSIAST MEDIA SUBSCRIPTION COMPANY

VP, Consumer Marketing	BOBBI GUTMAN

ISBN 1 929180 96 9

STYLE AND FLAIR

I REMEMBER THE FIRST TIME I SAW A LAYOUT BY LISA BROWN CAVENEY published in *Creating Keepsakes* Magazine. I was inspired by her clean sense of design, her stunning photographs, and her neatly hand-printed journaling.

Through her years as a published scrapbooker, Lisa's style and flair has continued to evolve. There's no question—Lisa has a great sense of design and photography. But her talents don't stop there! She has this way of drawing her reader into her scrapbook pages, thirsty for more.

Whether you've been following Lisa's work for years or have just discovered her, you'll be excited to find Lisa's signature touch everywhere in this book. She's got a special knack for creating beautiful pages with a minimum of supplies—and each page she creates tells a special story.

May Lisa's talent and genuine spirit inspire you as it has me for many years. Enjoy!

Becky Higgins

STEP-BY-STEP

WHEN I FIRST STARTED SCRAPBOOKING, I WAS AN ENGINEERING GRADUATE student with a limited amount of money to spend on scrapbooking supplies. I quickly realized I could stretch my scrapbooking budget by creating pages with just the basics: my photographs, cardstock and markers.

My early days of scrapbooking on a budget became the foundation of how I scrapbook today. Although I'm now an engineer (and it's no longer a splurge to buy a sheet of patterned paper or a piece of ribbon to add to a layout), I still design my layouts around the fundamentals: strong photographs, color, balance and composition. At the same time, I love the freedom to let my imagination run wild with the possibility of adding stickers, ribbon, metal embellishments, rubber stamps, acrylic paint, stitching and more to my pages.

In this book, I'll guide you through the process of creating layouts with just the basics as well as teach you how to "step up your scrapbooking" with one, two, three, four or more page embellishments. I'll teach you how to choose embellishments that help tell the stories on your pages by allowing your photographs and journaling to shine. Whether you love the basics or prefer a "sky's the limit" approach to scrapbooking, I hope this book will inspire you to create scrapbook pages you love.

Acknowledgements

I'd like extend a special thank-you to Angie Cramer, Allison Kimball, Shelley Laming and Denise Pauley for joining me on this journey with all their talent and inspiration. To my husband for his love and support. To my dad for continually serving as a rock in my life. To my sister for being there since the beginning. To my mom and grandparents for fostering my creative side as a little girl. To Georgene and Dorothy for adopting me as one of their own. To Anna, Carla, Erin, Sarah and Susan for being the greatest friends I could hope for. You all make my life richer, and I am a better person for knowing you.

Lisa Brown Caveney

HOW TO
USE THIS BOOK

Writing Step Up Your Scrapbooking reminded me that what I truly love about scrapbooking is the ability to document an event, to chronicle a memory, to share a story. Through experience, I've learned that I love creating pages that start with a core foundation (strong photographs, balanced composition) ... as well as having the creative freedom to pick and choose embellishments, and to discover the little touches that make my layouts feel complete.

Within each chapter, I'll share my tips on topics such as handwritten journaling and photography, and show you some fun ideas for mini book projects. You can also follow me on my Neighborhood Inspiration Walk as I point out the layouts and page elements that were inspired by things I found in my own neighborhood.

I also challenged designers Angie Cramer, Allison Kimball, Shelley Laming and Denise Pauley to create a range of layouts, from "just the basics" to "the sky's the limit." You'll find their inspiring and beautiful layouts within each chapter as well as their thoughts on how they created pages with a minimum of supplies.

I'd like to issue the same challenge to you. As you read through the chapters of this book, challenge yourself to create with just the basics. Look for ways to choose just one perfect embellishment for your pages. Play and experiment with matching a variety of supplies to create that finished look on your layouts. Involve your friends in a challenge to create layouts with 1, 2 3, 4 or more supplies. Stretch your creativity by turning cardstock into ribbon or by using markers and cardstock to design your own patterned paper. Learn how to add your personal touch to each page you design while keeping the focus on the story you want to share. You'll be stepping up your scrapbooking—and creating pages you love—in no time.

Contents

the
BASICS
of me

movies • national public radio • cooking • photography
entertaining • traveling • soda • sewing • reading • Scrapbooking

PASSPORT
United States
of America

THE PHILADELPHIA STORY
VERTIGO
CITIZEN KANE
Amélie
bread & tulips
POSTINO • POSTMAN

diet PEPSi Vanilla

SONY

CAT'S EYE   MARGARET ATWOOD
The Mysteries
Yann
Martel   Life of Pi
nning with Scissors
ARL S. BUCK   THE GOOD EAR
SOPHIE'S CHOICE
WILLIAM STYRON

THE
BASICS

What if ... you were stranded on a desert island and could only bring your most basic scrapbooking supplies along with you? Could you create beautiful scrapbook pages with only your photographs, cardstock and a pen? In this chapter, you'll discover that the answer is yes! Turn the page and learn how to design fantastic scrapbook layouts with just the basics.

hanauma bay

WHILE DEREK AND I WERE IN HAWAII WE WANTED TO GO SNORKELING SO WE WENT TO HANAUMA BAY. THE VARIETY OF FISH THERE WAS JUST AMAZING. THERE WERE TONS OF BRIGHTLY COLORED FISH WITH LOVELY STRIPES AND PATTERNS. WE LOVED IT SO MUCH THAT WE WENT BACK TO HANAUMA BAY ON TWO DIFFERENT DAYS.

HANAUMA BAY
Lisa Brown Caveney

Enlarge one beautiful photograph and use it as a background that extends across two scrapbook pages.

BAOBAB

Lisa Brown Caveney

Add journaling around your photographs to create frames.

FLIGHT

Lisa Brown Caveney

Direct your reader's eye across a two-page spread with an angled "v" cut from cardstock.

TUGELA GORGE HIKE

ON SATURDAY MORNING DEREK AND I CHECKED OUT OF MONTUSI AND DROVE TO ROYAL NATAL NATIONAL PARK. WE DECIDED TO HIKE THE 14 KM ROUTE FROM THE CAR PARK UP THE TUGELA RIVER GORGE. THE TRAIL WAS A NICE STEADY INCLINE ON THE WAY THERE. THE PATH HAD A MIXTURE OF WOODED AREAS PROVIDING SOME NICE SHADE AND SOME OPEN AREAS PROVIDING SOME GREAT VIEWS OF THE MOUNTAINS ESPECIALLY THE AMPHI-THEATER. THE ONLY DOWNSIDE WAS THAT THERE WERE A LOT OF BRUSH FIRES IN THE AREA MAKING THE SKY HAZY. THE TRAIL WAS PRETTY EMPTY SO THE HIKE WAS VERY QUIET AND PEACEFUL. 7/24

Lisa Brown Caveney

Layer traditional 4" x 6" prints over enlarged photographs.

Lisa Brown Caveney

Enlarge a macro-shot (such as the tree bark here) and use it as a page accent or photo mat.

HONU

Lisa Brown Caveney

Write captions directly on photographs.

OLD, NEW, BORROWED, BLUE

Lisa Brown Caveney

Create an eye-catching layout by cutting photographs and journaling blocks into horizontal strips.

10 TIPS FOR
NEATER HANDWRITTEN JOURNALING

When I first started scrapbooking, I didn't have a computer at home. I was in grad school at the time and just used my computer at school for research. Out of necessity, I started writing my journaling by hand. Although I now have a computer at home, I still journal by hand because I feel like I'm leaving a personal piece of me on my pages.

Being the detail-oriented engineer that I am, I like my journaling to look precise on my pages. When you're creating pages with just cardstock, photographs and a pen, your personal handwriting becomes an important page element—and you want it to look great. I've developed a few tips to tidy up my personal handwriting without losing my personal style. Here are 10 of my favorites:

1. Start with a good quality pen that writes in a fine line and doesn't skip. I like to use Zig Writers by EK Success and Gelly Roll pens by Sakura for most of my journaling.

2. Write slowly and deliberately. It helps me to think that I'm drawing each letter instead of quickly writing each letter.

3. Use a light box. I don't like drawing ruler lines on my layouts, so I use a light box and place a grid under my light-colored cardstock. Using the gridlines, I can to position my journaling where I want it to be.

4. Use a ruler as a journaling guide, but keep moving it down your page as you write each line of journaling. This will keep your journaling straight, but you won't have to erase any ruler lines.

5. By staggering the beginning of each line both the right and left sides of the text have a ragged look, filling the journaling space more uniformly.

6. Use the edges of your photographs as "journaling lines" and write your journaling on the edge, the bottom or even around your photograph.

7. Trace your journaling twice when writing on dark backgrounds with opaque markers. This will help your journaling stand out more.

8. Plan where you want to journal before you create your layout. Don't just try and squeeze it in at the end!

9. Use software to create a font in your own handwriting. A personal computer font will give you the look of your handwriting without the worry of trying to write neatly on your page.

10. Experiment with journaling directly on a photograph printed on matte paper.

CANADIAN THANKSGIVING

Lisa Brown Caveney

Cut symbols and icons from cardstock to create simple page accents.

canadian thanksgiving

LIVING IN THE UNITED STATES FOR OVER FIVE YEARS I KNOW THAT DEREK MISSES HIS HOME COUNTRY OF CANADA. I TRY TO BE SUPPORTIVE AND SO WE HAVE MADE IT A TRADITION TO CELEBRATE CANADIAN HOLIDAYS. OCTOBER BRINGS CANADIAN THANKSGIVING. IN CANADA IT IS CELEBRATED ON A MONDAY BUT BECAUSE WE DON'T GET THE DAY OFF WE USUALLY CELEBRATE ON THE SATURDAY BEFORE OR AFTER. WE INVITE OVER A BUNCH OF FRIENDS AND I MAKE A DINNER WITH ALL THE FIXINGS- TURKEY WITH STUFFING, MASHED POTATOES, GREEN BEANS, CRANBERRY RELISH, GRAVY, SWEET POTATOES, AND OF COURSE PUMPKIN PIE. WE ALWAYS HAVE A GREAT TIME HANGING OUT, CHATTING, AND EATING. EVEN THOUGH EVERYONE IS COMPLETELY STUFFED BY THE END OF THE EVENING WE END UP WITH A LOT OF LEFTOVERS SINCE I HAVE A TENDENCY TO OVERESTIMATE WHEN IT COMES TO THANKSGIVING. IT ACTUALLY WORKS WELL SINCE NOTHING TASTES BETTER THAN TURKEY SANDWICHES MADE FROM THANKSGIVING LEFTOVERS. CELEBRATING CANADIAN THANKSGIVING IS SURE TO BE A FUN TRADITION FOR YEARS TO COME.

SOUTH AFRICAN FAMILY

Lisa Brown Caveney

Design a back-ground page with just photographs.

SOUTH AFRICAN FAMILY

WHEN DEREK AND I GOT ENGAGED THE FIRST THING WE DECIDED WAS THAT WE WOULD HONEYMOON IN SOUTH AFRICA. DEREK'S PARENTS GREW UP IN SOUTH AFRICA SO ALL OF HIS GRANDPARENTS, AUNTS, UNCLES AND NEARLY ALL OF HIS COUSINS ARE IN SOUTH AFRICA SO WE FELT OUR HONEYMOON WOULD BE A PERFECT WAY FOR ME TO MEET THEM. DEREK AND I SPENT THREE WEEKS IN SOUTH AFRICA. DURING THE WEEK WE WENT TOURING AROUND THE COUNTRY SIGHTSEEING AND ON THE WEEKENDS WE SPENT TIME WITH DEREK'S FAMILY. DEREK'S PARENTS ALSO HOSTED A WEDDING BRUNCH FOR US WITH THE WHOLE FAMILY. DEREK'S FAMILY WAS SO KIND AND I LOVED GETTING TO KNOW THEM.

Lisa Brown Caveney

Design your own "patterned paper" by layering geometric shapes over a cardstock base.

GEAR

Lisa Brown Caveney

Experiment with the different looks you can create with your pens.

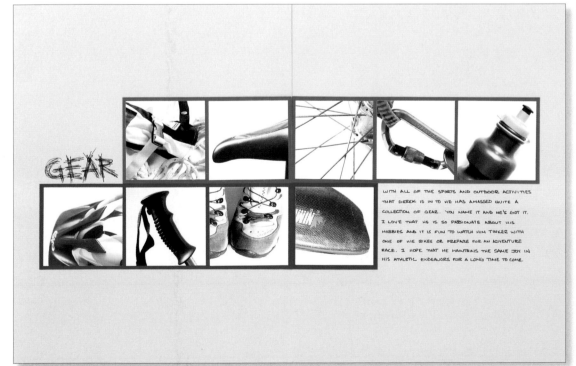

Neighborhood Inspiration Walk

When I need to find inspiration for a page design, one of my favorite things to do is to walk around my neighborhood. After I saw the roofline of this apartment building, I used white cardstock and the circle journaling block to mimic it. Try this exercise for yourself to see what inspiration you can find in your neighborhood!

VISITING KINGSTON IN OCTOBER WAS BEAUTIFUL. THE AIR WAS COOL AND CRISP. THE AUTUMN LEAVES WERE A LOVELY CONTRAST TO THE BLUE SKY AND THE WATER REFLECTED ALL THE SPLENDOR. WE HAD A GREAT TIME WALKING AROUND.

10/04

ctober

OCTOBER

Lisa Brown Caveney

kingston, ontario 2004

Look for a dominant curved line in your photographs (such as the dome here) and repeat it as a design element on your page.

DESIGNERS' SECRETS
WITH JUST THE BASICS

I love the challenge of creating a page with "just the basics" and always start with my photographs. I find they are the visual key to any layout and can easily fill most of the space on my page. I asked the other designers featured in this book to share their secrets for creating pages with just cardstock, photographs and a pen. Here's what they said.

Q: *What's your secret to designing a beautiful scrapbook layout with just cardstock, photographs and a pen?*

A. "When I was asked to create a layout with just cardstock, photographs and a pen, I decided to focus on the design and colors of the layout. When a layout is stripped of embellishments, the color and design become front and center. I tried to come up with unique designs and interesting color choices." —Angie Cramer

A. "My first thought was … argh! How in the world am I going to do this? I love to mix all sorts of patterns and colors and textures, so I knew this would be a challenge for me. I really had to think about how I scrapbook—I had to focus on colors and values and hues to create the movement and depth I wanted on my page. I was also inspired by my friend, Carrie Owens, to learn how to cut my own titles from cardstock." —Allison Kimball

A. "I've always liked creating layouts where my photographs and journaling shine, so I start by thinking about the story I want to share on my page and then build my page around it." —Shelley Laming

A. "I have to dig a little deeper, creatively. For example, I created a layout where I wanted to use ribbon. Because I didn't have ribbon, I had to improvise … to think of different ways to achieve the same look with cardstock. And you know what? It was pretty easy and fun! And economical!" —Denise Pauley

Denise Pauley

Write journaling directly on letters cut from cardstock.

Shelley Laming

Draw journaling lines directly on your cardstock with colorful pens.

Random Advice # 105

The source of love is deep in us. One word, one action, or one thought can reduce another person's suffering. One word can give comfort and confidence, destroy doubt, help someone avoid a mistake. One action can save a life. One thought can do the same because thoughts always lead to words and actions. If love is in our heart, every thought, word, and deed can bring a miracle. Because understanding is the very foundation of love. Words and actions that emerge from our love are helpful.
— Thich Nhat Hanh

1. "you got the bigger piece. No fair."

2. "Stop splashing soap in my eyes."

3. "You got to swing first. It's not fair."

4. "I don't want to be the prince. Why do I always have to be the boy?"

SILLY

How wonderful to have your best friend be your sister! You do everything together & miss one another when you are gone. This could almost be the most perfect relationship except for a few minor items.

SILLY

Allison Kimball
Photos by Jessi Stringham Photography

Color-block a background with textured cardstock that repeats two colors from your photographs.

7. "we already watched a movie you got to choose!"

6. "Mom, she's not being nice to me."

5. "Why are you always the boss of me?"

9. "Mom, I'm the only one cleaning the bedroom." "You ARE NOT!"

8. "It's mine! I had it first! Give it back!"

10. "My horse is going to be bigger than your horse." "No, mine is biggest."

11. "Does she have to play with me?"

"we will always be best friends, right?" "right! I love you!"
5-04

...this song makes me cry w... hear it. It reminds me of how proud of you and how blessed I am to be your... Your eyes are always so full of determination, happiness, mischief, hope and love that they're a glimpse right into your soul. This picture sums you up perfectly – a little sweet, a little silly – at age 6. ♥ mommy.

"In my daughter's eyes, everyone is equal. Darkness turns to light and the world is at peace. This miracle God gave to me gives me strength when I am weak. I find reason to believe in my daughter's eyes. And when she wraps her hand around my finger, it puts a smile in my heart... Everything becomes a little clearer... I realize what life's about. When I'm gone I hope you'll see how happy she made me. For I'll be there... in my daughter's eyes."
~Martina...

lift ❋

erin's eyes...

ERIN'S EYES
Denise Pauley

Draw flowers (or trace a pattern) onto cardstock and cut with scissors.

Cassidy and Chandler
5/2002

Among those whom I love, all of them make me laugh.
— W.H. Auden

CASSIDY & CHANDLER
Shelley Laming

Balance a single photo on a page with a cardstock accent/journaling block that is approximately the same size as your photograph.

AN UNEXPECTED HAPPY

Denise Pauley

Twist strips of cardstock and attach to a tag like ribbon.

BABOONS

Lisa Brown Caveney

Layer cardstock pieces within a two-page spread to create a two-toned back-ground for journaling and photographs.

Angie Cramer

Divide your page into thirds with a beautiful photograph.

Shelley Laming

Cut semi-circles from photographs and fill the open spaces with colorful cardstock circles.

DISNEYLAND

Lisa Brown Caveney

Trim strips of card-stock to assorted widths and layer them over cardstock to create a colorful striped background.

DISNEYLAND

GROWING UP GRANDPA WON WOULD ALWAYS TELL MISSY AND I THAT IF HE WON THE LOTTERY HE WOULD TAKE US TO DISNEYLAND. ANY LUNCH DATE WITH GRANDPA WAS SURE TO INCLUDE A STOP AT BERNIE SHULMAN'S TO BUY A LOTTERY TICKET. BOTH MISSY AND I WERE CONVINCED THAT SOMEDAY GRANDPA WOULD WIN AND WE WOULD BE OFF TO CALIFORNIA TO SEE MICKEY MOUSE. AS I GOT OLDER I REALIZED THAT GRANDPA WOULD NEVER WIN BUT THAT NEVER STOPPED OUR TRADITION. THE TIME I SAW GRANDPA BEFORE HE DIED WAS NO DIFFERENT. IT WAS DECEMBER 2000 AND GRANDPA TOOK ME OUT TO LUNCH BEFORE I HEADED BACK TO CALIFORNIA FOR SCHOOL. AFTER WE ATE WE STOPPED FOR A LOTTERY TICKET. AS HE HELD THE LOTTERY TICKET IN HIS HAND HE TOLD ME AS USUAL THAT IT WAS OUR TICKET TO DISNEYLAND. AFTER FOUR YEARS OF LIVING IN CALIFORNIA I HAD NOT BEEN TO DISNEYLAND. MY PLAN HAD ALWAYS BEEN TO TAKE GRANDPA WHEN I FINISHED SCHOOL AND GOT A JOB. UNFORTUNATELY HE PASSED AWAY A YEAR BEFORE I GRADUATED. I FINALLY MADE UP MY MIND TO GO TO DISNEYLAND DURING THE SUMMER OF 2005. I DECIDED TO GO ALONE BECAUSE IT JUST DIDN'T FEEL RIGHT TO GO WITH ANYONE OTHER THAN GRANDPA. ONCE I ENTERED THE PARK I WISHED THAT I HADN'T COME. I WAS OVERWHELMED WITH THOUGHTS OF GRANDPA AND WISHING HE WAS THERE. AFTER A LITTLE WHILE MY UNEASINESS FADED AS I REALIZED HE WAS WITH ME IN SPIRIT. I ENDED UP HAVING MORE FUN THAN I ANTICIPATED AND IT WAS A GREAT WAY TO SPEND THE DAY REMEMBERING GRANDPA.

LAUGHTER

Lisa Brown Caveney

Tear and weave cardstock strips together to create a dimensional page background.

laughter

Allison Kimball

Stack vertical strips of extra cardstock along the bottom of your page to create a border.

Angie Cramer

Trace waves onto cardstock and free-hand cut them with a pair of scissors.

Neighborhood Inspiration Walk

When I need to find inspiration for a page design, one of my favorite things to do is to walk around my neighborhood. When I saw this wrought iron gate, I replicated the iron work with a pink swirl and created the woven paper strip background based on the metal grillwork. Try this exercise for yourself to see what inspiration you can find in your neighborhood!

Angie Cramer

Print a symbol, such as a parenthesis mark, in reverse onto cardstock and cut it out with scissors as a page element.

TRIUMPHANT

Allison Kimball

Repeat an image on your page, such as the bathroom tiles here, with cardstock squares.

6 THINGS TO TRY
FROM THIS CHAPTER

As a scrapbooker, I'm always excited to try something new on my pages. Here are six assignments that will allow you to play with the ideas I presented in this chapter:

1. Challenge yourself to create a page that uses only cardstock, photographs and markers.

2. Try one of the handwritten journaling techniques listed on page 15.

3. Create a page border that's made only from strips of leftover cardstock.

4. Look at magazines for ideas on how to create well-designed layouts that use only photographs and words.

5. Create a title from cardstock using one of the ideas on page 33.

6. Play with your markers. Use them to design your own patterned paper or to practice handwriting titles.

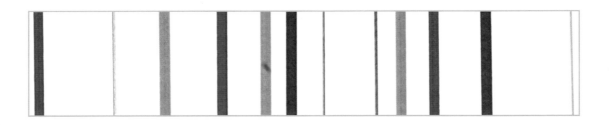

MINI
BOOK

In order to make a mini book with just the basics and no embellishments, I knew
I'd need to be strong on my fundamentals: color, composition, and balance. I started
this mini book with a basic design scheme I could repeat on each page. I wanted to
add a bit of extra color to the design, so I created the "patterned paper" on each
page with markers and strips of paper.

SNAPSHOTS AT BONDI
Lisa Brown Caveney

TAKE ANOTHER LOOK ...
AT THESE GREAT TITLES!

As I worked on this chapter, I realized the impact a title cut from cardstock can have on a page. I love to use my Fiskars micro-tip scissors to cut out my cardstock titles because they're sharp and have a great point.

You can create a cardstock title in several ways, but my favorite three are:

1. Use a lettering template. Trace the letters onto the back of your card stock and cut them out. Tip: *I've discovered some fantastic templates in the sign-making section of my local craft store.*

2. Print and hand-cut your title. I like to choose my favorite computer font, type it out, reverse it, print it on the back of my cardstock, and cut it out.

3. Sketch your own letters. Look at other lettering options, such as stickers and rubber stamps, and use them as inspiration to sketch your own titles onto cardstock.

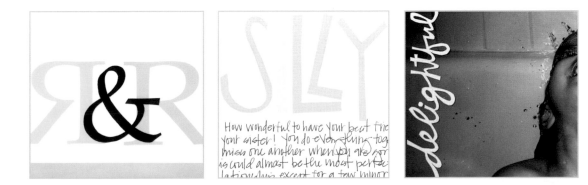

PLUS 1
ELEMENT

Chapter Two

So, you've started with the basics, and you're ready to step it up a level—just one step at a time. In this chapter, you'll learn how to create beautiful layouts with cardstock, photographs, a pen ... and one embellishment of your choice. Ready to start accessorizing? Here's how.

ONEONEONEONEONEONEONE
NEONEONEONEONEONEONEON
EONEONEONEHE'STHEONEONEONE
ONEONEONEONEONEONEONEO
NEONEONEONEONEONEONEON
EONEONEONEONEONEONEONE
ONEONEONEONEONEONEONEO

MAUNAWILI FALLS

Cross-stitch a border to unify the elements on your layout.

Lisa Brown Caveney
+1: embroidery floss

DEREK AND I WOKE UP TO A
WET RAINY MORNING ON FRIDAY. WE
DELIBERATED A BIT AND THEN
DECIDED TO GO FOR A HIKE. WE
CHOSE TO TAKE THE MAUNAWILI
DEMONSTRATION TRAIL TO THE
MAUNAWILI CONNECTOR TO THE FALLS
FOR A ROUND TRIP OF EIGHT
MILES. DURING THE HIKE IT
SHOWERED ON AND OFF BUT THE
SCENERY WAS BEAUTIFUL. BUILT
INTO THE BASE OF THE WINDWARD
KOOLAU CLIFFS THE TRAIL OFFERED
VIEWS OF WATERFALL CHUTES
AND THE OLOMANA PEAKS.
WHEN WE GOT TO MAUNAWILI FALLS
THEY WERE LOVELY. DEREK STRIPPED
DOWN TO HIS SHORTS AND WENT
FOR A SHORT SWIM AND THEN
CLIMBED TO THE TOP OF THE FALLS.
IT WAS SO PEACEFUL AND RELAXING.
AFTER ENJOYING A LIGHT SNACK
DEREK AND I HEADED BACK UP
THE TRAIL THROUGH THE LUSH
VEGETATION BACK TO THE TRAILHEAD.
FEBRUARY 4, 2005

NORWEGIAN SUN

Lisa Brown Caveney
+1: patterned paper

Unify the elements on your layout by pulling cardstock colors from your patterned paper.

norwegian sun

DEREK AND I DECIDED TO SPEND OUR 2004 THANKSGIVING HOLIDAY ON A CRUISE. WE CHOSE TO TAKE A WESTERN CARIBBEAN ITINERARY OFFERED ON THE NORWEGIAN SUN. WE HAD AN AMAZING TRIP VISITING THE CAYMAN ISLANDS, HONDURAS, BELIZE, AND MEXICO. WE ALSO HAD A LOT OF FUN ON BOARD EATING GOOD FOOD, RELAXING IN LOUNGE CHAIRS, READING, AND WALKING ALONG THE PROMENADE DECK IN THE EVENING. IT WAS A FABULOUS TRIP. NOV. 2004

Neighborhood Inspiration Walk

When I need to find inspiration for a page design, one of my favorite things to do is to walk around my neighborhood. This gate looked like a sun to me, and I thought it would make a perfect accent for my layout about our cruise on the Norwegian Sun. Try this exercise for yourself to see what inspiration you can find in your neighborhood!

FOSTERS

Lisa Brown Caveney
+1: foam stamps

Feature colorful photographs on a neutral background to allow your pictures to shine.

BEING BACK AT DUKE FOR REUNION WEEKEND MEANT VISITING FAVORITE PLACES WITH GOOD FRIENDS. ON SATURDAY, I HAD LUNCH WITH SARAH, SUSAN, AND ANNIE AT FOSTER'S MARKET. IT WAS A GORGEOUS SPRING DAY SO WE ATE OUTSIDE IN THE SUN. GOOD FRIENDS, GOOD FOOD, GOOD WEATHER — WHO COULD ASK FOR ANYTHING MORE? APRIL 17, 2004

FOSTERS

Lisa Brown Caveney
+1: rub-ons

Create continuity on a layout by repeating one element (here, the title) across the length of your page.

AFTER OUR VISIT AROUND THE ISLAND OUR DRIVER DROPPED US OFF AT THE DOCK WHERE WE BOARDED AND DEREK AND I GOT SOAKED. THE COLORS OF THE OCEAN AND SKY LOOKED LIKE THEY WERE WE GOT OUR SNORKEL GEAR AND HEADED INTO THE WATER. THE SANDBAR ALLOWED US TO STAND WITH STINGRAYS. IT WAS SO NEAT TO WATCH THEM. THEY WERE INCREDIBLY GRACEFUL NO HAD WERE VELVETY SOFT ON THEIR UNDERSIDE BUT ROUGH LIKE SANDPAPER ON TOP. DEREK HAD A CHANCE STINGRAYS WAS AN AMAZING EXPERIENCE – MY FAVORITE IN THE CAYMAN ISLANDS. I COULD HAVE

A BOAT TO TAKE US TO STINGRAY CITY. WHEN THE BOAT SPED UP IT KICKED UP A LOT OF SPRAY FROM A POSTCARD, WITH THE TEAL CONTRASTING AGAINST THE BABY BLUE. WHEN WE ARRIVED WAIST DEEP BUT THE VIEW WAS SO MUCH BETTER UNDERWATER. THE AREA WAS TEEMING A HABIT OF BRUSHING UP AGAINST PEOPLE'S LEGS LIKE THEY WEREN'T EVEN THERE. THEY TO FEED ONE OF THE STINGRAYS A PIECE OF SQUID FROM HIS HAND. INTERACTING WITH THE STAYED IN THE WATER WITH THE STINGRAYS FOR HOURS. NOVEMBER 22, 2004

SIGNING
THE REGISTER

Lisa Brown Caveney
+1: computer font

Use photographs in the place of patterned paper to create an elegant look for your layouts.

SNORKELING IN COZUMEL

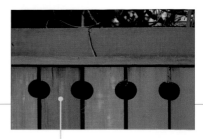

Lisa Brown Caveney
+1: patterned paper

Lighten up darker photographs by matting them on white cardstock.

Neighborhood Inspiration Walk

When I need to find inspiration for a page design, one of my favorite things to do is to walk around my neighborhood. When I saw this wooden fence, it reminded me of portholes, and I knew it would be perfect for my snorkeling photos. Try this exercise for yourself to see what inspiration you can find in your neighborhood!

GRAND CANYON

Lisa Brown Caveney
+1: rub-ons

Try printing photographs at panorama size to add a different look and feel to your layouts.

7 TIPS FOR
GREAT PHOTOGRAPHS

I've discovered that the key to a strong layout is a strong photograph. When I take pictures, I always think about taking a variety of shots. I try to capture close-ups, mid-range shots and wide-angle shots so I have a quite a few choices to feature on my scrapbook pages. One of my favorite tips? I like to use an enlarged photograph of a wide-angle shot (to provide an overview of my page theme and set the tone for the page) with a 4" x 6" close-up shot (to provide detail).

1. I always take lots of photographs. This way, I'm sure to get a few great ones that really capture the moment.

2. I like to take close-up photographs of details such as textures or architectural elements. I often use these photographs as background paper or page accents.

3. I try to include people in my layouts for perspective. For example, I was really struck by the size of the rock formations at Red Rock. By including some hikers in the photo, my readers will have a sense of size that the photograph might not otherwise convey.

4. I don't scrapbook all of my photographs. Sometimes, I find that just one or two strong photographs are a more effective way to document a memory.

5. I've learned how to take photographs through trial and error. When I look at my photographs, I examine them for what works and what doesn't.

6. If you have a friend or family member who takes great pictures, ask her to explain how she captures such engaging images.

7. Walk around your neighborhood and look for images that catch your eye. The photographs may inspire a design element on a future scrapbook page.

zipline

AFTER WALKING AROUND TOWN EXPLORING ROATAN A BIT DEREK AND I WENT ON A ZIPLINE CANOPY TOUR. IT WAS REALLY COOL. AFTER GETTING ON OUR HARNESS, HELMET, AND GLOVES WE WERE SET TO GO. THERE WERE THIRTEEN PLATFORMS WITH ELEVEN ZIPLINES. IT WAS SO AWESOME TO BE HIGH UP IN THE CANOPY AND SPEEDING ON THE ZIP LINE WAS QUITE A RUSH. I JUST LOVED IT! 11-23-04

ZIPLINE

Lisa Brown Caveney
+1: stickers

Try a vertical orientation for your title and journaling.

JULEHYGGE

Lisa Brown Caveney
+1: stickers

Consider non-traditional color schemes (here, brown, red, and white) for your holiday layouts.

A GOOD DAY

Lisa Brown Caveney
+1: stickers

Create a clothing-inspired background for your page.

Azay le Rideau

Cheverny

Villandry

CHATEAUX OF THE LOIRE VALLEY

Amboise

Chenonceau

Chambord

Lisa Brown Caveney
+1: computer font

Type photo captions directly on your photos and print them out.

GROTE MARKT

GRAND PLACE
GROTE MARKT

BRUSSELS' MAIN SQUARE, GROTE MARKET (GRAND PLACE), WAS A FABULOUS SIGHT. LOCATED IN THE HEART OF BRUSSELS' OLD TOWN IT WAS A HUB OF ACTIVITY WITH TONS OF PEOPLE AND A FLOWER MARKET. THE ARCHITECTURE OF THE BUILDING LINING THE SQUARE WAS ELEGANT AND IMPRESSIVE. GROTE MARKET SERVED AS BRUSSELS' MARKET SQUARE EVOLVING FROM A PLACE WHERE FARMERS AND MERCHANTS SOLD THEIR WARES IN OPEN AIR STALLS TO A PLACE FILLED WITH CAFÉS AND SHOPS FULL OF BELGIAN SPECIALTIES LIKE GAUFRES (WAFFLES), MUSSELS, FRIES, LACE, AND CHOCOLATE. WITH ITS THREE HUNDRED FOOT TALL TOWER THE STADHUIS (TOWN HALL) IS THE MOST PROMINENT FEATURE OF THE SQUARE. IT WAS WHERE THE CITY COUNCIL MET TO GOVERN THE TOWN AT A TIME WHEN MUCH OF EUROPE WAS RULED BY ARISTOCRACY OR CLERGY. THE GUILD HALLS SURROUNDING THE SQUARE WERE AMAZING TO ME. I LOVED THEIR ORNATE ROOFLINES TOPPED WITH STATUES. THEY DATE BACK TO 1695 WHEN THEY WERE REBUILT AFTER BEING LEVELED BY LOUIS XIV'S TROOPS. I REALLY ENJOYED SOAKING IN THE ATMOSPHERE OF GROTE MARKT. BEAUTIFUL PLACE! JUNE 2004

Lisa Brown Caveney
+1: punch-outs

Repeat an ornate element from your photographs as an accent on your page.

Neighborhood Inspiration Walk

When I need to find inspiration for a page design, one of my favorite things to do is to walk around my neighborhood. The buildings of Grote Markt are so ornate that I needed something ornate for my layout as well. My layout came together when I came across this decorative bracket. Try this exercise for yourself to see what inspiration you can find in your neighborhood!

tabyana beach

TABYANA BEACH

Lisa Brown Caveney
+1: buttons

Add square buttons to a mosaic to add texture and interest to a layout.

after our zip line trip through the jungle canopy we spent the rest of the afternoon at Tabyana Beach. The sky was an amazing shade of blue and the water was a beautiful teal. We went snorkeling and had fun checking out all the amazing sea life. After our snorkel we relaxed in some beach chairs in the shade and Derek even took a nap. It was incredibly relaxing and peaceful out to laying in the warm weather. It was like a little slice of heaven. And I was sad to take the bus back to the ship. 11-23-04

DESIGNERS' SECRETS ...
TO COLOR CHOICES!

When designing pages with only one embellishment, color becomes a key part of your layout design. I usually spend a lot of time playing with the colors on my layout to find just the right combination. I asked the contributing designers in this book to share their favorite tips for choosing colors to feature on their layouts. Here's their advice:

Q: *When creating a page with limited supplies, what are your tips for choosing colors?*

A. "I heard this color advice on a decorating show: Always add a touch of black to every room because it helps to anchor your eye. This same principle can be applied to designing scrapbook pages. Adding a bit of black to a page can give it the finishing touch it needs to look complete." —Angie Cramer

A. "I like to start with the clothing of a focal person in a picture. Choose colors based on the colors the person is wearing and your reader's eye will be directed to that person." —Allison Kimball

A. "I like to create moods on my pages, and color is such an important part of creating a mood or feel for a page. I like to start with the story I want to tell and then choose colors that will evoke a mood or feeling." —Shelley Laming

A. "I look for colors that will complement my photographs, make them pop and call out my favorite elements on the page. I like to find a highlight color in my photos to mix and match. Or, sometimes I'll start with a neutral shade to allow all my photographs to stand out." —Denise Pauley

This was CUTE... I was in the after school carpool lane and I see you 'be-boppin' up the sidewalk. I squinted to try and make out your new hair-do. I said, "Hey Sarah! Who did your hair?!" You very proudly exclaimed, "Me! I did it!" I couldn't stop grinning... because of your independence ...your total confidence...but most of all—that sweet smile!

NEW HAIR-DO

Shelley Laming
+1: ink

Adhere inked strips of cardstock in varying widths as a colorful page embellishment.

DEAR MAMA WINNIE

Denise Pauley
+1: computer font

Write your journaling in the form of a letter to a favorite stuffed animal.

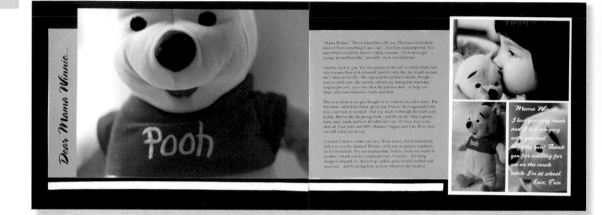

SPRING SUMMER AUTUMN WINTER

Angie Cramer
+1: computer font

Color words (spring, summer, winter, fall) to match corresponding seasonal photographs.

gg roomies '04
Tara + Margie + I go way back...getting to room with them at the Wisconsin garden girl get-together was a blast! It made a great weekend even better. I love my girls!

GG ROOMIES '04

Shelley Laming

+1: ink

Create your own embellishments for your pages by freehand drawing or tracing designs onto cardstock.

READ

Allison Kimball
+1: ribbon

Add extra photographs to your layout by attaching them to tags and slipping the tags into pockets.

4.

(before going to...

(too relaxing...

5.

6.

(with your sisters)

(100.) Dragons...
...izza (101.)

(133.) Island of the blue dolphin... (134.)
the Great...

...zzz up...
...is...
...erensh...
one
(78.

In an adventure
of fantasy or
exploration. You have
traveled around the
world, across galaxies
and through history
all in one year!

What a wonderful
treasure for your
mind.

(ps. thankfully you
like to share your passion
with your sisters!)

GLOW

Shelley Laming
+1: staples

Staple page accents to your layouts.

glow
shine
illuminate
gleam
radiate
shimmer

Shea - summer '04

K

Allison Kimball
+1: patterned paper

Capture your child's unique personality with a layout that showcases her range of expressions.

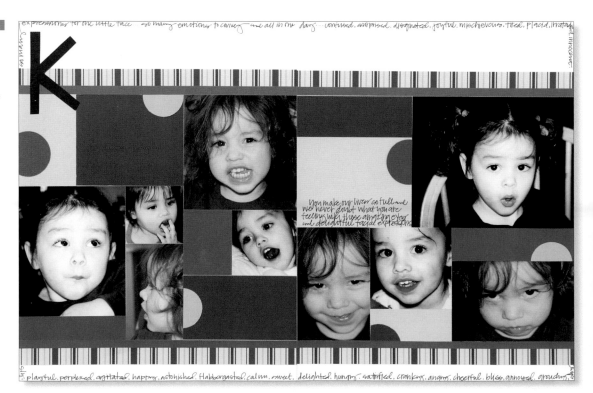

painful memories

The truth about wakeboarding. It's not always fun being dragged behind a boat and being subject to all manner of physical abuse. Every now and then a bad wipe-out can really make a guy wonder what if it's worth it. This was one of those days. A nasty fall that quickly ended a summer afternoon of fun. A reminder that it's not always an enjoyable ride but sometimes it can be downright painful.

Gary – summer 2004

PAINFUL MEMORIES

Angie Cramer
+1: computer font

Rip a line down the center of a layout to represent a painful moment.

THIS SMILE

Shelley Laming
+1: ribbon

Attach vintage ribbon to a layout to add a touch of sweetness and charm.

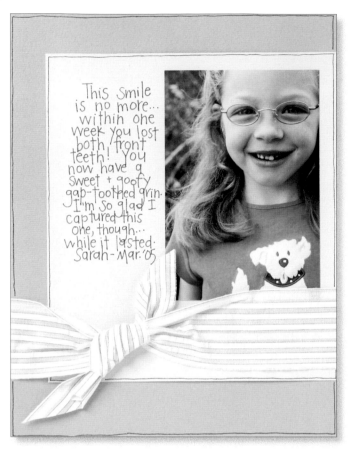

This Smile is no more... within one week you lost both front teeth! You now have a sweet + goofy gap-toothed grin. I'm so glad I captured this one, though... while it lasted. Sarah - Mar. '05

COLORFUL YOU

Angie Cramer
+1: computer font

Digitally tint a favorite photograph in several different hues and use it as a design element on your page.

COLORFUL YOU

YOU ARE ADVENTUROUS LIKE RED. YOU ARE HAPPY LIKE PINK. YOU ARE ENERGETIC LIKE YELLOW. YOU ARE CONTENT LIKE BLUE. YOU ARE OPTIMISTIC LIKE WHITE. YOU ARE OUTGOING LIKE ORANGE. YOU ARE THOUGHTFUL LIKE GREEN. YOU ARE VIBRANT LIKE VIOLET. YOU ARE A CLASSIC LIKE BLACK. YOU ARE ALL THAT AND SO MUCH MORE. COURNTEY 04

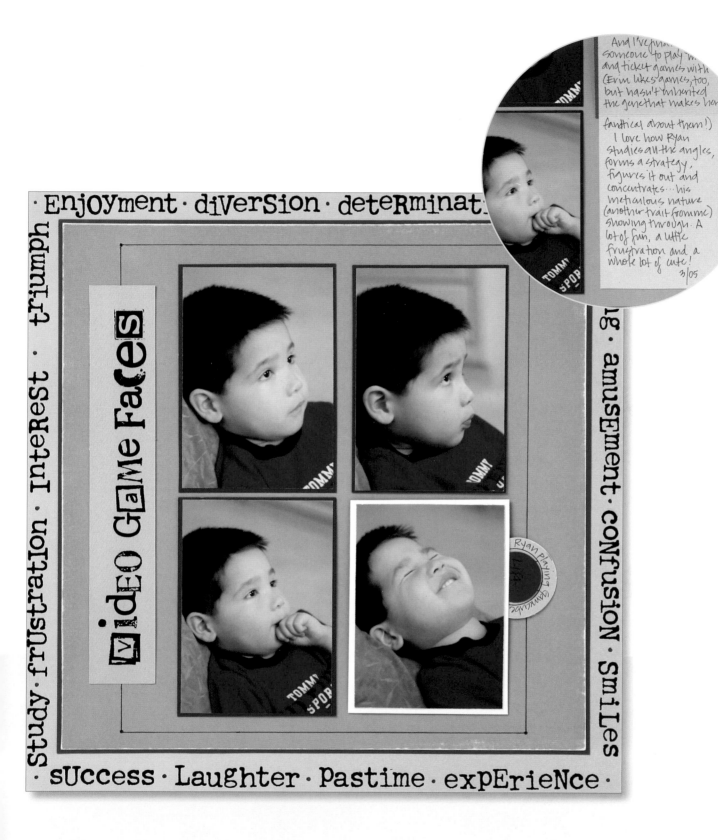

VIDEO GAME FACES

Denise Pauley
+1: rub-ons

Use rub-ons to create a matching page title and border.

BABY

Allison Kimball
+1: stitching

Create a warm, comfortable feeling by purposely stitching crookedly on your layout.

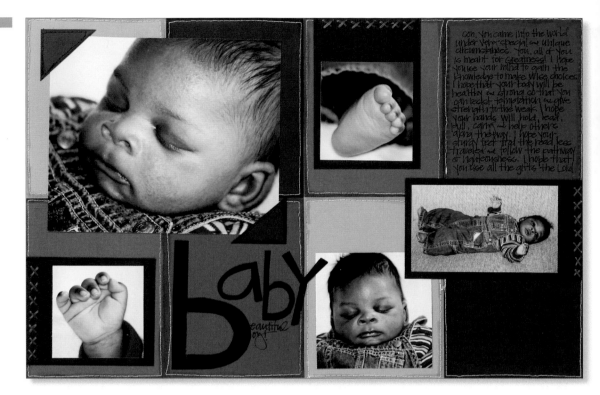

2004 ELECTION

Lisa Brown Caveney
+1: ribbon

Transfer a party theme (here, red, white and blue) to a scrapbook page documenting the same event.

6 THINGS TO TRY
FROM THIS CHAPTER

As a scrapbooker, I'm always excited to try something new on my pages. Here are six assignments that will allow you to play with the ideas I presented in this chapter:

1. Take a walk around your neighborhood and look for inspiration you can transfer to your scrapbook pages.

2. Have a photograph printed at a panoramic size and feature it across both pages of a two-page layout.

3. Experiment with stickers and rub-ons or printing, writing or stamping titles or captions directly on your photographs.

4. Find a colorful element that you like in a photograph, such as the lilacs in my "Fosters" layout on page 38, and repeat it as a focal color on your page.

5. Challenge yourself to tell a story on a page that includes just photographs and photo captions.

6. Design a page background that's inspired by a piece of clothing.

MINI
BOOK

I'm always looking for new ways to display my photographs and memories. Sometimes, you can tell a story just by featuring beautiful photographs in an elegant album. This album is simply a visual summary of our honeymoon in South Africa and features photographs with rubber-stamped captions.

SOUTH AFRICA COFFEE TABLE BOOK

Lisa Brown Caveney
+1: stamping

BAOBAB TREE

BABY BABOON

HOUT BAY HARBOUR

ATLANTIC SURF

TAKE ANOTHER LOOK ...
AT THESE LITTLE DETAILS

When designing a page with just a few supplies, you can achieve a strong visual impact with just the smallest of details. Take a second look at the little details that my designers and I added to our pages in this chapter:

GLOW
Shelley Laming
The detail: outlined text box
What it does: emphasizes and grounds the text

BABY
Allison Kimball
The detail: stitched photo corner
What it does: adds extra emphasis to the focal-point photo

GG ROOMIES
Shelley Laming
The detail: inked flower petals
What it does: defines the flower accent

ZIPLINE
Lisa Brown Caveney
The detail: ripped photo edge
What it does: creates a sense of movement on the page

2004 ELECTION
Lisa Brown Caveney
The detail: "election" strip added to title
What it does: completes the title in a small amount of space

PAINFUL MEMORIES
Angie Cramer
The detail: cardstock strip in letters
What it does: draws your eye through the title and layout

PLUS 2

Chapter Three

ELEMENTS

You started with the basics and stepped it up once. Ready to step it up again? In this chapter, you'll learn how to create beautiful scrapbook pages with the basics (cardstock, photographs and a pen), plus two additional page elements.

I LOOK FORWARD TO THE TIME WHEN DEREK AND I START A FAMILY BUT FOR NOW I'LL ENJOY THIS TIME WITH just the 2ofus

GAUDI

Lisa Brown Caveney
+2: patterned paper, stickers

Fit 12 photographs on an 8 ½" x 11" layout by cutting them into squares.

GAUDI

MY FAVORITE PART ABOUT VISITING BARCELONA WAS SEEING THE ARCHITECTURE OF ANTONIO GAUDÍ. ERIN AND I SOUGHT OUT AS MANY OF HIS BUILDINGS AS WE COULD VISITING CASA BATLLÓ, CASA MILÀ, SAGRADA FAMILIA, PALAU GÜELL, CASA CALVET, AND PARK GÜELL. THE BUILDINGS WERE SO INNOVATIVE IT WAS HARD TO FATHOM THAT THEY WERE BUILT ONE HUNDRED YEARS AGO. I LOVED THE MOSAICS, THE IRONWORK, THE SCULPTURE, EVERYTHING! GAUDÍ WAS A VISIONARY AND IT WAS AMAZING TO SEE HIS WORK.

MEADOW WOODS

Lisa Brown Caveney
+2: punch, eyelet letters

Pull out your old punches and find new ways to use them as page accents.

PHD

Lisa Brown Caveney
+2: patterned paper, paint

Paint letters onto cardstock and write your journaling over the painted images.

SOO LINE

When Grandpa Overbye was little he and his brothers would take the train to spend the summer with his grandparents on their farm. That was the beginning of his lifelong love of trains and the Soo Line in particular. When I found this vintage railway map of N. Dakota I knew Grandpa would love it.

Lisa Brown Caveney
+2: computer font, memorabilia

Add meaning to your pages with memorabilia.

DEUTSCHES MUSEUM

Being engineers Derek and I had a lot of fun at the Deutsches Museum in Munich. The museum traces the history of science and technology. With ten miles of exhibits there was so much to see — historic boats, cars, trains, aircraft, spaceships, mining, the harnessing of wind and water power; hydraulics, musical instruments, printing, chemistry, computers, astronomy, clocks, and much more. It was so much that it was overwhelming and we had to pick out things to see since we could not see it all in one day. Derek's favorite part was seeing the car and train exhibits. I really liked the musical instruments and the exhibits on classical physics. There were all sorts of experiments to play with that illustrated physics principles. Derek and I had a great time exploring the Deutsches Museum.

Lisa Brown Caveney
+2: patterned paper, stickers

Stagger alphabet stickers across the middle of your page to create a title that directs the eye across the design.

Lisa Brown Caveney
+2: patterned paper,
rubber stamps

*Add curved lines to
your layout to create
visual interest.*

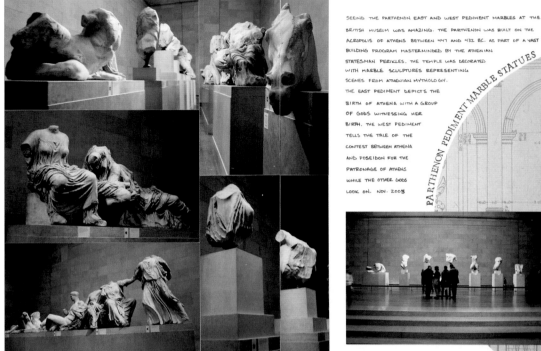

TOGETHER

Lisa Brown Caveney
+2: twill tape,
metal embellishments

*Trace letters onto
cardstock and use an
X-acto knife to cut
out the inside of each
letter.*

Neighborhood Inspiration Walk

When I need to find inspiration
for a page design, one of my
favorite things to do is to walk
around my neighborhood. I
found my inspiration in this
sign, featuring ampersand-
entwined initials. I cut out a
cardstock ampersand and
paired it with alphabet twill
tape highlighting our initials.
Try this exercise for yourself to
see what inspiration you can
find in your neighborhood!

Lisa Brown Caveney
+2: stickers, vellum

Illustrate a favorite recipe with macro shots of the finished product.

Lisa Brown Caveney
+2: stickers, rub-ons

Freehand-cut a swirled design to pull your reader's eye across the page.

RED ROCKS

Lisa Brown Caveney
+2: stickers, fiber

Journal directly on a photograph that's been printed on matte paper.

WHILE DEREK AND I WERE IN LAS VEGAS WE DECIDED TO HEAD TO RED ROCKS TO GO HIKING. MY FAVORITE PART WAS VISITING THE CALICO HILLS. THE COLOR OF THE ROCKS WAS SIMPLY STUNNING AND THE ROCK FORMATIONS WERE REALLY BEAUTIFUL. IT WAS SO NEAT TO CLIMB AROUND THE SANDSTONE AND KEEP DISCOVERING NEW SIGHTS AROUND EACH CORNER.
I JUST LOVED IT!

CHICAGO IN JULY FO[...]
so many momentous highlights...
1. MEETING JANET. After five-plus years of near daily e-mails, we finally, finally met. It's always amazing how comfortable it is to meet an Internet pal in real life...how much we already "know" each other and how easy it is to hang out, as if we'd seen each other millions of times. Shopping, eating, sightseeing, *walking*, watching a movie... good times.
2. CATCHING UP WITH OLD FRIENDS, MEETING NEW ONES. Always love the chance to see the CK crew and other scrapbookers that I've come to know as friends. So touching that we've connected and bonded through this hobby that has become a way of life for us.
3. SEEING SEURAT'S LA GRANDE JATTE IN PERSON. Breathtaking. One of my all-time favorite works of art... something I never thought I'd see. I'd completely forgotten that it was housed at the Art Institute of Chicago...and we happened to visit the week the gallery was hosting the "Making of La Grande Jatte." So serendipitous. Inspiring. Heavenly. Seeing it up close simply fueled my drive to create those little scrapbook layouts that brought me to Chicago in the first place.
4. RIDING THE EL. Fun, a tad confusing (and could those doors close any faster?!)...and very ER-like! ☺
5. ME TIME. I don't travel that often, but when I do, I love it...a chance to relax and fully recharge. And my favorite part is seeing the kids' faces when I walk in the door...BLISS!

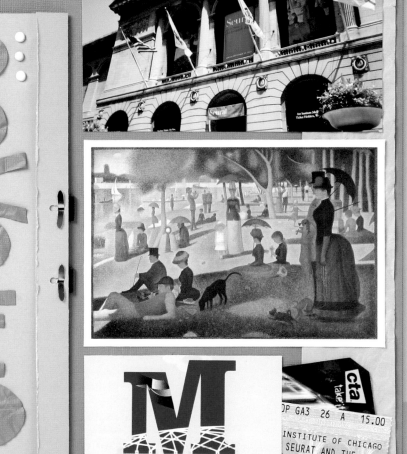

Millennium Park
JULY 16-18, 2004

cta

OP GA3 26 A   15.00

INSTITUTE OF CHICAGO
SEURAT AND THE
OF LA GRANDE JATTE
EEN 12:00PM-12:30PM
RIES CLOSE: 4:45 PM
NDAY JUL 18 2004

CHICAGO

Denise Pauley
+2: brads, computer fonts

Turn decorative brads upside down to create journaling closures.

10 TIPS FOR USING CARDSTOCK ON YOUR PAGES

Next to my photographs, cardstock is the main staple of my scrapbook supplies. Here's a list of my favorite ways to use cardstock when I'm creating layouts:

1. Create titles using cardstock. It's easy to do this with a template. Just use the template to trace letters onto cardstock and then cut letters out with an X-acto knife or a pair of scissors.

2. Mat photographs to make them stand out from the background. For extra emphasis you can double-matte your photographs with contrasting cardstock.

3. Create a picture frame of cardstock around the outer edge of a layout.

4. Make borders with cardstock and punches.

5. Weave cardstock strips together to create a textured background.

6. Trace a map onto cardstock and cut it out (think of it as a large die-cut shape).

7. Cut out a large monogram letter or number from cardstock.

8. Cut simple shapes from cardstock—for example, a flag, a flower or a sun. Look at die cuts and stickers for inspiration ideas.

9. Add strips of accent color with cardstock to make the colors in your photos pop.

10. Make a mosaic with a square punch and cardstock. Choose a pattern for your mosaic and then punch out the appropriate number (and colors) of squares needed to compose your design.

CROSS COUNT

1 death valley 2 las vegas 3 zion n.p. 4 bryce canyon

CROSS COUNTRY

Lisa Brown Caveney
+2: stickers, metal embellishments

Fit eight scenic photographs on your page by trimming photos into 2" vertical strips.

RY DAD AND I LOVE GOING ON ROAD TRIPS TOGETHER. WHEN I FINISHED UP MY MASTER'S THESIS DAD FLEW OUT TO CALIFORNIA AND WE DROVE TO OHIO STOPPING AT SEVERAL NATIONAL PARKS. SINCE IT WAS FEBRUARY THERE WERE FEW TOURISTS AND WE HAD A BLAST! FEB. 2002

5 dead horse point s.p. 6 canyonlands n.p. 7 arches n.p. 8 denver

DESIGNERS' SECRETS ... CHOOSING THE PERFECT EMBELLISHMENTS

How do you choose the embellishments that are just right for your page? Does it really matter which embellishments you choose? My answer is yes. Think of a really great outfit you love, and think about how you can change the look by selecting flats over heels, or a simple pendant over a string of beads. Here, the contributing designers share their tips for choosing the best embellishments for your pages.

Q: *What's your secret to choosing the best embellishments for your scrapbook pages?*

A. "I think it's important to allow yourself to experiment and to not be afraid to mix and match page elements. For example, Christmas doesn't have to be red and green. It also doesn't have to include embellishments of Santa, reindeer and stockings by the fireplace. Have fun and experiment with unique (even unexpected!) embellishments on your pages." —Angie Cramer

A. "To help me learn where (and why!) to place embellishments on my pages, I've studied the principles of design. Accents can be an important way to illustrate your story, but they can also help move your reader's eye from one part of your page to the next. When I choose embellishments, I make sure each element somehow contributes to my layout design." —Allison Kimball

A. "When choosing and/or creating an embellishment for a page, I like to start by thinking about the look and feel I want to create. For example, for a sweet and rustic look, I might freehand-cut hearts from chipboard, cover them with fabric scraps and ink the edges." —Shelley Laming

A. "I love the different looks I can create on my pages with supplies. I like to be able to pick and choose just the right embellishments to make a page feel complete. When I choose embellishments, I try and choose items that will help me visually communicate the story on my page, whether it's flowers and ribbon on a 'girly' page or metal embellishments on a page about my son." —Denise Pauley

Shelley Laming
+2: fabric, ink

Freehand-cut four hearts and cover them with scraps of fabric to create a sweet page accent.

daddy + sarah

Sarah: it warms my heart how close you + your dad are. Mar.'05

But, the reality of this "blurred" photo (and the entire roll) is what happens when I sit on the ground with camera in hand. "A FULL ON ATTACK! You come running, crawling and moving as fast as you can to climb on my lap, jump on my back, or even to sit on my head.

Allison Kimball
+2: patterned paper, stitching

Feature slightly blurred photographs on a page—the movement may tell an important part of your story!

ATTACK

SIX

Allison Kimball
+2: patterned paper, brads

Maximize layout space by cropping your photographs to fit your page.

"Death by chocolate"... that is the best way to describe your birthday this year! Chocolate, chocolate, chocolate! If you could have you probably would have chosen something chocolatey for breakfast, but then you would have missed your favorite eggs, bacon & hashbrowns.

You are one of the first to turn six in our kindergarten class me that seems to be a pretty big deal to you. You wanted to bring ice cream sandwiches to share with your class. Uncle Thomas called you first thing in the morning before you left for school me that made you quite happy.

Each birthday party yielded art supplies... lots me lots of different supplies. From paper, to crayons, to paints me color pencils. It was no dream come true as you stated at the end of the festivities. I'm glad you had fun! Happy Birthday sweet girl! I can hardly believe another year is gone! I love you! mommy

TWEENDOM

Shelley Laming
+2: stickers, ink

Place your letter stickers in a crooked fashion to add a fun and whimsical touch to your layout.

SUGAR & SPICE

Allison Kimball
+2: patterned paper, stickers

Journal about two different aspects of your child's personality.

Angie Cramer
+2: computer fonts, ribbon

*Group photographs
and titles into a
visual square.*

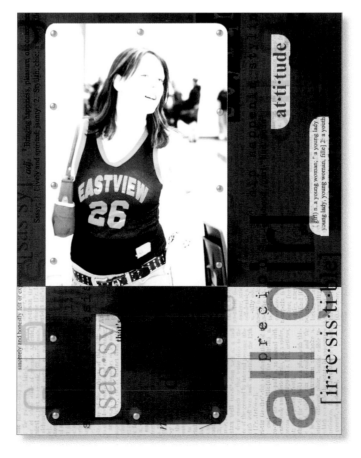

Angie Cramer
+2: preprinted transparency,
brads

*Round the top
corners of your
photograph to add
a whole new look to
your page design.*

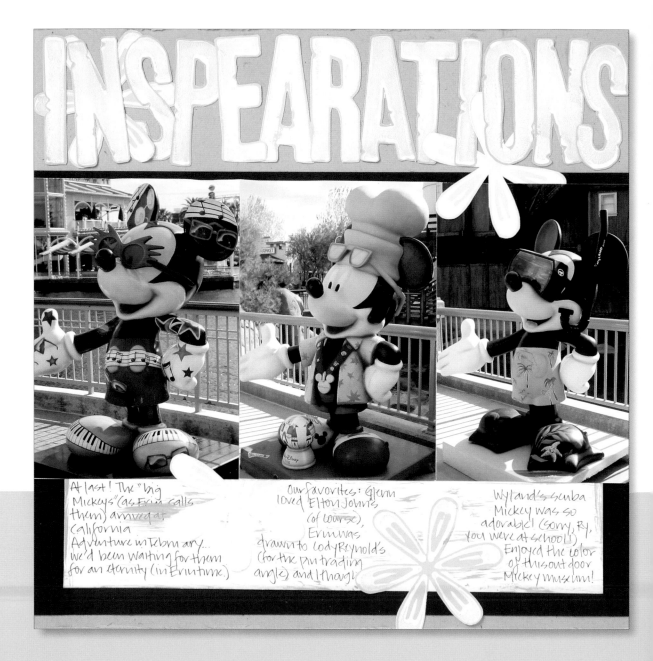

At last! The "big Mickeys" (as Erin calls them) arrived at California Adventure in February... We'd been waiting for them for an eternity (in Erin time).

Our favorites: Glenn loved Elton John's (of course), Erin was drawn to Cody Reynold's (for the pin trading angle) and I thought

Wyland's scuba Mickey was so adorable! (Sorry, Ry, you were at school!) Enjoyed the color of this outdoor Mickey museum!

INSPEARATIONS

Denise Pauley

+2: acrylic paint, foam stamps

Add texture and color to your journaling space by applying acrylic paint after writing your journaling.

Angie Cramer
+2: patterned paper,
computer font

*Ground your
accents within your
layout with a card-
stock frame.*

happynineteenthbirthday!

Allison Kimball
+2: patterned paper,
chipboard alphabet

*Thread paper ribbons
through punched
holes in cardstock.*

I would have never guessed that our christmas card would have received such an overwhelming response. The truth is I was in a rush & nothing profound came... so this is what was leftover.

I heard back from so many of our friends, relatives, acquaintances about how much they had laughed me how they had shown everyone who came to their homes. I was so embarrassed! I certainly wasn't prepared for this. I even learned that a news reporter was quite upset with chad because she hadn't shown him the card in time to use on his news story. (I was relieved!)

So my next big question is how can I top this accident next year? Have I created an expectation I can not meet. The pressure! Let's hope someone says something funny funny next years photo shoot.

Our annual quest for the perfect family photo was no different this year than in the past. It was filled with stress, chaos and uncooperative participants.

Unnamed child: "Mom, couldn't we just get a photo off the internet?"

Mom: "You mean, someone else's photo?"

Unnamed child: "Sure, there has to be tons of better-looking families than us and it's already done."

Mom: "What do we say in the card?"

Unnamed child: "We could just tell them that the perfect family photo cannot happen with us, but these people sure do look nice."

From our chaotic home to yours we wish you a very,

Merry Christmas

CHRISTMAS CARD

Allison Kimball
+2: patterned paper, greeting card

Think outside the box and decorate your layouts with items such as greeting cards and gift wrap.

On the layout:

PLAY!
SCORE!
WIN
COUNT!!

tHe aRcade...tHe mecca oF Fun.
RYan has a New favoRite...though what he
really loves is watching the numbers on the
scoreboard change...he'll even score on his own goal.

R loves
air hockey!
(sort of...)

PLAY, SCORE, COUNT
Denise Pauley
+2: patterned paper, ink

Trim photographs to fit a montage—or create a similar effect with a photo-editing program, such as Adobe Photoshop.

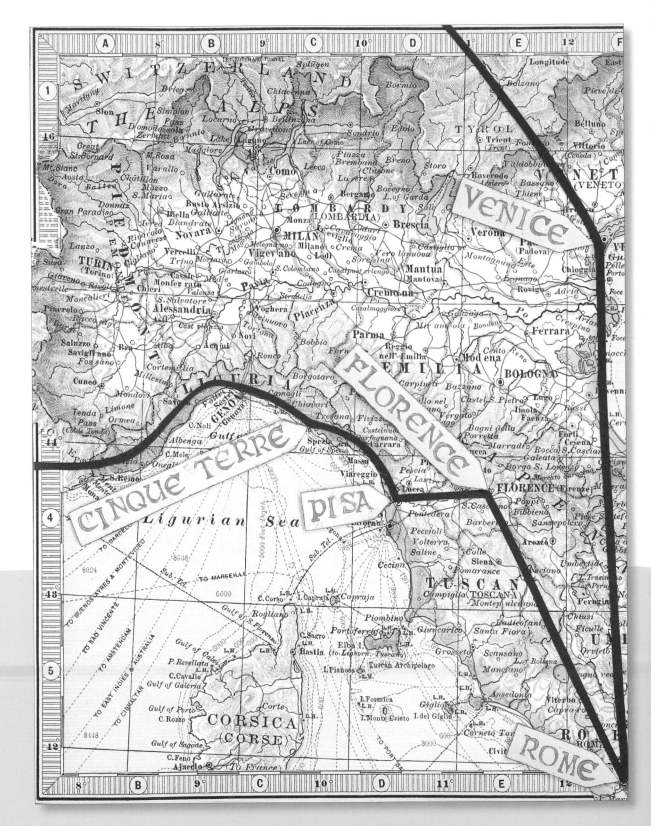

ITALY

Lisa Brown Caveney

+2: rubber stamps, wrapping paper

Cut a piece of map-inspired wrapping paper to create a unique page background.

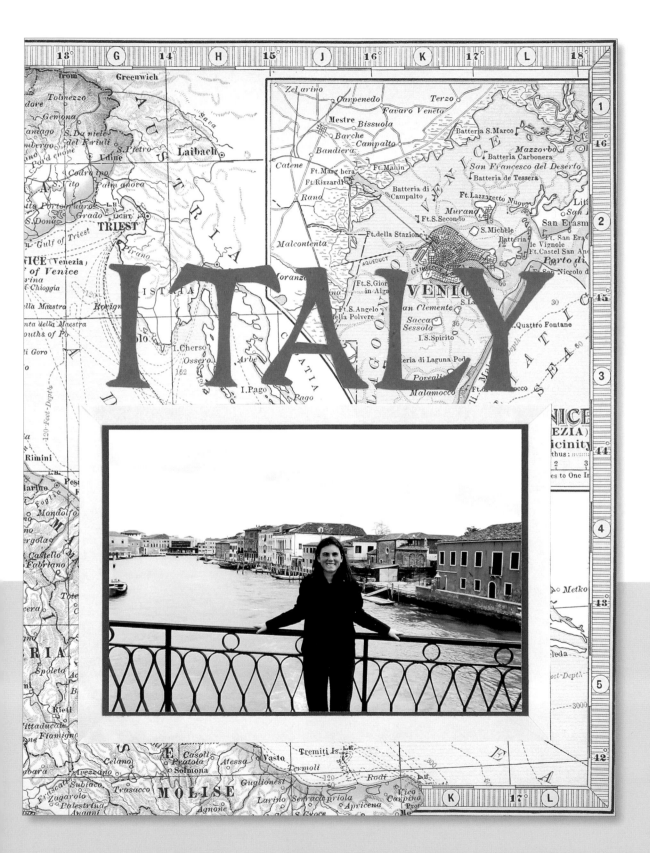

I LOVE TO WRITE

Denise Pauley
+2: patterned paper, stitching

Ask your child to handwrite journaling on a layout that showcases a special skill.

The week that we camped at Lake Newell was one of the coolest weeks of the entire summer. We only made it to the beach a couple of times when the sun peeked out.

Jenna, Albert, Karen

The wind was so cold on the day these pictures were taken that we had to find a sheltered spot to play. Rick and Karen's campsite was where we ended up spending the bulk of the day.

Essentials: cards, scorepad candy and blue whales.

Around the table - Harry, Allison, Audrey, Gary, Jenna, Albert, Karen.

Camping just wouldn't be camping without games to play. Board games, card games, tile rummy and chicken foot are a few of our favorites.

Every year we learn a new card game and this year was no different. 2004 was the year of "Farmer's Poker". We all caught on quickly and couldn't get enough of it. Talk about addiciting!

The beauty of this game is that a large number of people can play at one time including the younger kids. It's the perfect game for a large crowd.

2004 was also the year of lousy camping weather so we played ALOT of Farmer's Poker. We pretty much played all day with the odd break in between to eat or go for a walk.

We are so addicted to playing games that we take cushions along for sitting on. Some games can go on for hours which can lead to sore butts from the sitting on the hard wooden benches.

Of course our game playing wouldn't be complete without snacks to keep us going. Fuzzy peaches, trail mix, peanuts, spitz, fruit snacks and blue whales are necessities.

It's not uncommon to have several games going on at the same time. All you need is an empty picnic table and a few willing players and you're all set.

fun and games

Farmer's Poker is actually alot like rummy. The goal is to group all your cards into sets and get them down on the table as fast as possible. You can also add cards to other players cards that have been laid on the table.

Any cards left in your hand after someone has gone out count as points against you. You must have a minumun of 3 cards in a set to lay it down. Two's and Jokers are wild.

There are 8 rounds in each game and each player is allowed 10 buys from the discard pile per game. A buy gives you the top card of the discard pile as well as the top 3 cards in the draw pile. You can use a maximum of 3 buys at one time.

The game starts out easy but gets harder with each round so it's best to save a couple of buys for the last round or you'll be in trouble.

Angie Cramer
+2: computer fonts, computer paper

Highlight photographs on your page with computer-drawn circles.

Carly
Abby
Chandler
05.02

tight end of the school year hugs.

they know Chandler will be in louisiana for the whole summer soon.

Shelley Laming
+2: greeting card, ink

Cut apart a greeting card and use it to accent your layout.

I don't have a lot of photographs of my dad, so when I found this series of him with his parents at age 16 weeks, I wanted to do something special. First, I made an accordion out of tan cardstock and placed the photographs on one side. Then, I cut out letters spelling my dad's name from a piece of vintage-reproduction wrapping paper and placed them on the other side.

WALTER BROWN, JR.

Lisa Brown Caveney
+2: vintage wrapping paper, twill tape

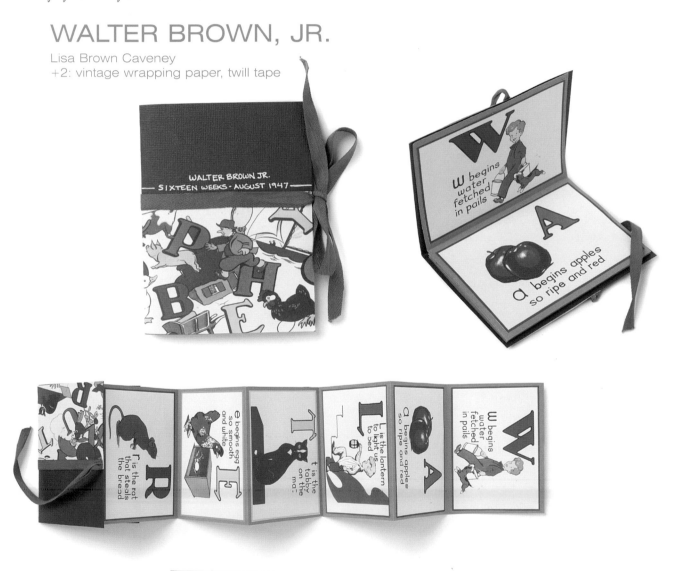

I travel quite a bit for work, so I made this tiny album (it's only about 2 ½" x 2 ½")
to take with me on trips when I miss my husband, Derek.

DEREK

Lisa Brown Caveney
+2: metal letter, rub-ons

I made this album to chronicle our first home together. I sketched a rough floor
plan of the apartment and made a two-page spread about each room.

OUR FIRST HOME

Lisa Brown Caveney
+2: acrylic paint, metal key charms

erin + andy

ERIN AND ANDY WANTED TO HAVE A SMALL DESTINATION
THEY CHOSE TO GET MARRIED AT LOUGH CUTRA
THE LAKE. SINCE I WAS HEADING TO IRELAND
THEIR FAMILIES AT LOUGH CUTRA A FEW DAYS BEFORE
THERE. THE WHOLE TIME WE KEPT JOKING
AND ANDY GOT MARRIED OUTSIDE NEXT TO
TRADITIONS IN IT. AFTER THE CEREMONY
IRISH BLESSINGS AND TOASTED THE HAPPY
ANY IRISH DANCING BUT WE ALL TRIED OUR BEST

ERIN + ANDY

Lisa Brown Caveney
+2: stickers, computer clip art

Look for unique borders and page accents in your computer clip art.

WEDDING AND SINCE BOTH OF THEM HAVE IRISH HERITAGE IRELAND WAS A PERFECT CHOICE.
CASTLE IN GORT IN COUNTY GALWAY. IT WAS JUST BEAUTIFUL THERE WITH THE CASTLE OVERLOOKING
FOR THE WEDDING I DECIDED TO TOUR AROUND A BIT AND THEN MET UP WITH ERIN, ANDY, AND
THE WEDDING. IT WAS FUN TOURING AROUND THE GROUNDS OF THE CASTLE AND STAYING
THAT WE COULD GET USED TO CASTLE LIVING. THE WEDDING WAS LIKE A FAIRY TALE. ERIN
THE CASTLE. THE CEREMONY WAS REALLY SWEET AND THE PRIEST INCLUDED SEVERAL IRISH
WE HEADED INSIDE TO THE DINING ROOM FOR A FABULOUS DINNER. DURING DINNER WE READ
COUPLE. AFTER DINNER WE HAD FUN DANCING TO AN IRISH BAND. NONE OF US REALLY KNEW
TO DO A JIG. IT WAS A TRULY FABULOUS WEDDING FOR A TRULY FABULOUS COUPLE. JUNE '04

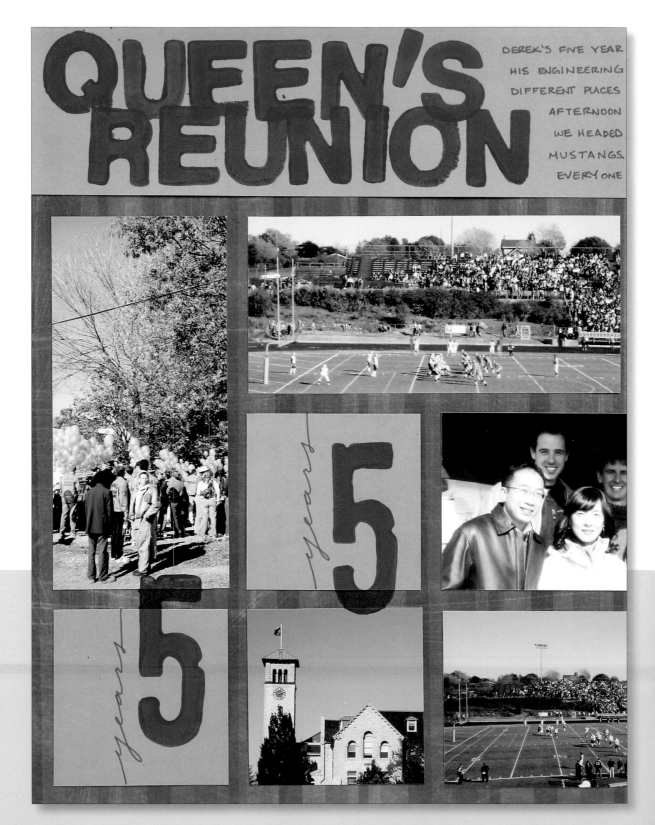

QUEEN'S REUNION

Lisa Brown Caveney

+2: patterned paper, stamps

Feature your school colors on a layout that celebrates a reunion, a graduation or another school-related event.

UNIVERSITY REUNION AT QUEEN'S WAS A LOT OF FUN. WE MET UP WITH A BUNCH OF
BUDDIES FOR MOST OF THE WEEKEND. DEREK SHOWED ME ALL HIS OLD HAUNTS, THE
HE LIVED, AND THE BUILDINGS HE TOOK CLASSES IN. WE WENT TO RITUAL ON FRIDAY
AND THE APPLIED MATH ALUMNI SOCIAL ON SATURDAY MORNING. ON SATURDAY AFTERNOON
TO THE STADIUM TO WATCH THE GOLDEN GAELS TAKE ON THE U. OF WESTERN ONTARIO
QUEEN'S PUT UP A GOOD FIGHT FOR A WHILE BUT GOT ROUTED IN THE END. SUNDAY MORNING
LEFT AFTER BREAKFAST AND DEREK AND I WALKED AROUND KINGSTON BEFORE OUR FLIGHT. 10/04

6 THINGS TO TRY
FROM THIS CHAPTER

As a scrapbooker, I'm always excited to try something new on my pages. Here are six assignments that will allow you to play with the ideas I presented in this chapter:

1. Instead of trimming your photographs into squares, experiment with trimming them into vertical and horizontal rectangles, like I did on my "Queen's Reunion" layout on page 94.

2. Create a layout based on a blurred photograph that shows movement.

3. When spelling out a title with stickers or rub-ons, create a fun sense of movement by placing your letters crookedly—on purpose!

4. For a unique and custom look on your page, cut page backgrounds and/or accents from gift wrap and greeting cards.

5. Ask family members to handwrite journaling on your page.

6. Grab an inkpad and experiment with inking the edges of a journaling box or the edge of an accent.

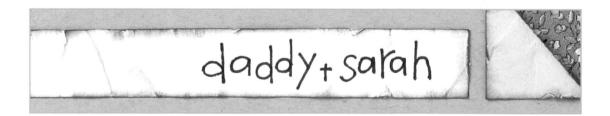

TAKE ANOTHER LOOK ...
AT THESE CREATIVE ACCENTS

CARLY, ABBY & CHANDLER
Shelley Laming
The accent: colorful squares
Where it came from: Shelley cut the front of a greeting card into squares

ITALY
Lisa Brown Caveney
The accent: background paper
Where it came from: Lisa cut the background paper from gift wrap

CHICAGO
Denise Pauley
The accent: journaling closures
Where it came from: Denise turned decorative brads upside down

WALTER BROWN, JR.
Lisa Brown Caveney
The accent: alphabet letters
Where it came from: Lisa cut the letters from vintage gift wrap

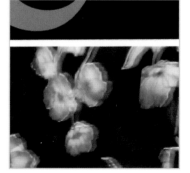

LET'S DANCE
Angie Cramer
The accent: flowered "patterned paper"
Where it came from: Angie digitally sampled a fabric swatch from her daughter's dress

SOO LINE
Lisa Brown Caveney
The accent: "Soo-Line" patterned paper
Where it came from: Lisa created the paper digitally by filling a red text box with white text

PLUS 3

Chapter Four

ELEMENTS

Did you know that adding accents to your pages is as easy as one, two, three? In this chapter, we'll teach you how to mix and mingle three accents on your layouts. Ready to get started? Here's how.

three day weekend

3

Grand Canyon

Sunset Crater

Montezuma's Castle

Wupatki

DEREK HAD NEVER BEEN TO ARIZONA BEFORE SO WE DECIDED TO SPEND A THREE DAY WEEKEND THERE. OUR FIRST STOP WAS THE GRAND CANYON. WE WENT ON A SIX MILE HIKE TO SKELETON POINT AND BACK. LUCKILY WE HAD FINISHED OUR HIKE AND WERE BACK ON THE BUS BEFORE IT STARTED TO POUR. THE NEXT DAY IT WAS STILL RAINING AS WE VISITED SUNSET CRATER AND WUPATKI NATIONAL MONUMENT BUT THE WEATHER CLEARED WHEN WE WERE AT MONTEZUMA'S CASTLE. THE PARKS WE VISITED WERE ALL LOVELY DESPITE THE WEATHER. WHAT A GREAT WEEKEND. SEPTEMBER 2004

DINGLE BIKE RIDE

Lisa Brown Cavenoy
+3: patterned paper, stickers, rub-ons

Create extra journaling space on your layout by justifying your photographs and title toward one side of your layout.

BY THE TIME I WALKED INTO TOWN FROM MY HOSTEL FOUND A PLACE TO STOW MY BAG AND RENTED A BIKE I ONLY HAD FIVE HOURS TO RIDE THE 29 MILE RIDE I HAD PLANNED ON BEFORE CATCHING THE LAST BUS OUT OF TOWN THAT AFTERNOON. I WASN'T SURE I COULD DO IT BUT I WAS DETERMINED. I LEFT DINGLE TOWN AND RODE PAST VENTRY BAY STOPPING TO SEE DUNBEG FORT WHICH DATES BACK TO THE IRON AGE. I NEXT STOPPED JUST UP THE ROAD AT THE BEEHIVE HUTS OR CLOCHANS. AFTER ADMIRING THE STONE STRUCTURES AS WELL AS THE VIEW I CONTINUED ON TO SLEA HEAD WHERE I HAD SOME STUNNING VIEWS OF THE BLASKET ISLANDS. I HAD BEEN SNACKING ON SOME THINGS I HAD PACKED WITH ME BUT I WAS DYING FOR A COLD DRINK SO I BOUGHT A BOTTLE OF WATER AND A SCONE IN BALLY-FERRITER AND THEN CONTINED ON TO REASC MONASTERY. DATING FROM THE 6TH - 12TH CENTURIES THE MONASTERY HAD INCORPORATED CELTIC FEATURES INCLUDING A STONE PILLAR FROM C. 500 BC. I NEXT HEADED FOR GALLARUS ORATORY. BUILT 1300 YEARS AGO IT IS ONE OF IRELAND'S BEST PRESERVED EARLY CHRISTIAN CHURCHES. AT THIS POINT I GOT LOST TRYING TO FIND KILMALKEDAR CHURCH AND HAD TO BACK TRACK A BIT. I DEBATED JUST SKIPPING IT SINCE TIME WAS RUNNING SHORT BUT IN THE END I DECIDED I WAS TOO CLOSE TO GIVE UP AND CONTINUED ON. WHEN I GOT TO THE CHURCH I HAD BEEN RIDING UPHILL FOR A FEW MILES AND HAD A FEW MORE CONTINUING ON UP TO GO. I WAS EXHAUSTED BUT I KNEW THAT THE LAST THREE MILES BACK INTO TOWN WERE ALL DOWNHILL SO I KEPT GOING REPEATING "THREE MILES DOWNHILL" TO MYSELF. WITH RELIEF I REACHED THE CREST AND COASTED BACK INTO DINGLE TOWN. 6/04

FREEDOM TO TRAVEL

Lisa Brown Caveney
+3: patterned paper,
transparency, rub-ons

*Photocopy stamps
from your passport
onto photo paper to
make your own
unique background
paper.*

CSR

Lisa Brown Caveney
+3: patterned paper,
computer font, rub-ons

*Replace traditional
photo captions with
borders featuring
family members'
names.*

The wall around the city was one of my favorite parts about visiting Rothenburg. The wall stretches about one and a half miles and provided wonderful views of the city. It was fun walking around above the hustle and bustle of the city. One of the towers, Rödertor, was open to climb up. It was 135 steps but the view from the top made it all worth it. I could see the whole city and several major Rothenburg highlights from the top of Rödertor. It was a beautiful way to see the city after we had seen it up close on the street. July 2003

ROTHENBURG
ob der tauber

Lisa Brown Caveney
+3: fabric letters, stickers, stamps

Piece together several photos to create your own panoramic page border.

CHRISTMAS 2004

Lisa Brown Caveney
+3: ribbons, corrugated cardstock, stickers

Combine photographs from different events on one layout.

CHRISTMAS 2004

DUTCH TULIPS

Lisa Brown Caveney

+3: patterned paper, letter stickers, rub-ons

Feature bright and colorful photographs on a neutral background.

DEREK AND I VISITED AMSTERDAM IN AUGUST SO THERE WERE NO TULIPS BLOOMING AT THE TIME BUT THERE WERE BULBS FOR SALE ALL OVER THE CITY. THE BLOEMENMARKT (FLOWER MARKET) ALONG THE SOUTH BANK OF THE SINGELGRACHT WAS STUNNING WITH ITS VARIETY OF BULBS, SEEDS, CUT FLOWERS, AND PLANTS FOR SALE IN ITS GREENHOUSE SHOPS. TULIPS IMPORTED FROM TURKEY IN THE SIXTEEN HUNDREDS GREW WELL IN THE SANDY SOIL OF THE DUNES AND RECLAIMED LANDS OF HOLLAND. BY THE 1630s THE COUNTRY WAS IN THE GRIP OF TULIP MANIA WITH BULBS SELLING FOR AS MUCH AS A HOUSE SOMETIMES. IN 1637 THE TULIP MARKET CRASHED BUT THEY REMAINED A STAPLE OF THE DUTCH ECONOMY. TODAY HOLLAND IS STILL A MAJOR EXPORTER OF FLOWERS. IF DEREK AND I DIDN'T LIVE IN AN APARTMENT I WOULD HAVE BROUGHT HOME SOME BULBS TO PLANT. 8/04

DUTCH tulips

Lisa Brown Caveney
+3: patterned paper,
watercolor paint, rub-ons

*Draw or trace a map
of the places you've
traveled and add it to
your layout as a
page accent.*

THANKSGIVING ABROAD

Lisa Brown Caveney
+3: patterned paper,
ribbon, stamps

*Extend the line of
your focal-point
photo by placing a
ribbon underneath it
that spans the length
of your layout.*

ALHAMBRA

7 TIPS FOR
USING COLOR ON YOUR PAGES

Color is a great tool for reinforcing the theme of a layout, as well as drawing focus and making the layout visually interesting. Here are seven of my favorite tips for choosing colors for my scrapbook pages:

1. When choosing cardstock for a layout, start by looking at your photographs. Pull colors from your photos that will reinforce the tone you want to create on your layout.

2. The most obvious color choice for a layout isn't always the best. Don't be afraid to experiment with different colors.

3. Bright and busy pieces of cardstock or patterned paper should be used sparingly on your layouts.

4. You can tone down a bright piece of patterned paper by placing a sheet of vellum over the pattern.

5. Do you have busy photographs? Choose a neutral-colored background.

6. Play with color schemes that include one light color and one dark color (for example, try pear green with brick red, or light apricot with royal blue).

7. Dark photographs often call for light backgrounds. For example, if you've got dark hiking photographs, don't feature them on a dark evergreen background. Try a pale avocado or cerulean green instead.

Neighborhood Inspiration Walk

When I need to find inspiration for a page design, one of my favorite things to do is to walk around my neighborhood. When I saw this awning, I knew the painted swirl would make a perfect accent for a layout with my photos of the Banzai Pipeline. Try this exercise for yourself to see what inspiration you can find in your neighborhood!

BANZAI PIPELINE

Lisa Brown Caveney
+3: patterned paper, acrylic paint, rub-ons

Paint a swirl onto your background paper and use it as a guide for your title letters.

SCANDINAVIAN DESSERTS

Lisa Brown Caveney
+3: patterned paper,
file folder, rub-ons

Tuck recipes into a file folder on your layout.

CROSSWORD

Lisa Brown Caveney
+3: patterned paper,
rub-ons, clips

Think about present-ing your titles in a creative way that helps tell the story on your page.

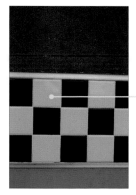

Neighborhood Inspiration Walk

When I need to find inspiration for a page design, one of my favorite things to do is to walk around my neighborhood. This tile and stucco wall reminded me of crossword puzzle squares—a perfect border for a layout about my grandma's love of crossword puzzles. Try this exercise for yourself to see what inspiration you can find in your neighborhood!

georgene has been a part of my life for as long as i can remember. she is like an aunt to me she's helped me out by giving me good advice and helping me through as i struggled with a difficult situation. she is one of the most generous people i know always giving of herself. after retiring as a teacher she has filled her time with volunteer work. she and aunt dorothy play music at a retirement home. georgene also volunteers at a hospital helping out with newborn babies. i've known georgene for the past quarter century and i hope that she continues to be an integral part of my life in the future.

GEORGENE

ADOPTED FAMILY

i'm not actually related to aunt dorothy but she's been like an extra grandmother to me for my whole life. she's incredibly giving and quite a spunky lady. aunt dorothy has retired several times only to go back to work again part time because she is bored. she's finally retired again but is helping out at a hospital and playing music at a retirement home. new things never phase aunt dorothy. she is up to date on all sorts of computer things and has email friends all over. i feel blessed to know and love her.

DOROTHY

Lisa Brown Caveney
+3: metal letters, mesh, computer font

Divide your layout in half with a title that extends across both pages.

EASTER EGGS

easter

EGGS

Lisa Brown Caveney
+3: patterned paper, ribbon, rub-ons

Look through your supplies for ribbon accents to add a finishing touch to your layouts.

DESIGNERS' SECRETS ...
PAGE DESIGN TIPS

As a scrapbooker, I like to repeat items on my pages and incorporate little tricks into my layout design. I asked the contributing designers in this book to share one of their favorite scrapbooking tips. Here's what they said:

Q: *What's one of your favorite design tips for creating great layouts?*

A. "Add extra dimension to your layouts by printing your journaling text and/or titles onto a transparency instead of printing directly on cardstock. I've found that text printed on a transparency seems to have a crisper and brighter look to it."
—Angie Cramer

A. "Maximize the space in your scrapbook by including lots of photographs of the same event on a double-page spread. Don't be afraid to cut your photographs to fit the design, theme and mood of your layout." —Allison Kimball

A. "It doesn't matter if you're scrapbooking an event photograph or a moment photograph—think about the emotional impact you want your layout to have on your reader. Do you want her to smile? Do you want her to laugh? Do you want her to understand? Do you want her to make a connection?" —Shelley Laming

A. "When you're trying to line up photographs across a two-page spread, use a yardstick. It's easy to position it where the "line" of your photographs should fall. Then, you can simply move your photographs, borders, journaling blocks and embellishments to the top of the yardstick so they're aligned properly on your page."
—Denise Pauley

Shelley Laming
+3: brads, stamps, acrylic tiles

Design a series of layouts around the advice you want to share with your children.

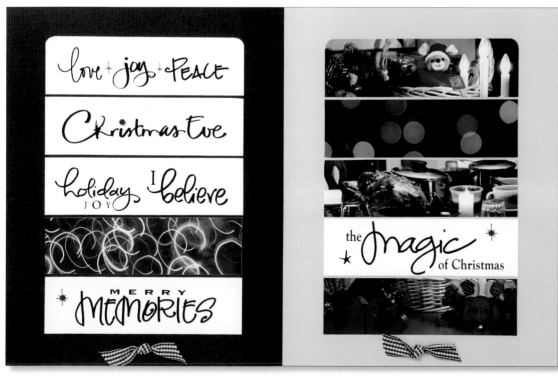

Angie Cramer
+3: rub-ons, brads, ribbon

Place three brads in a visual triangle to help move your reader's eye across your layout.

THE MINUTE HAND

Denise Pauley
+3: printed transparency, flower trim, stamps

Stamp lyrics from a favorite song onto your layout.

Sisters now... but it wasn't always so. At the ages of 11 and 6 you were united. It makes me smile when I hear one of you refer to the other as "my sister"... leaving off the "step" part. 03/05

SISTERS NOW

Shelley Laming

+3: patterned paper, photo corners, ink

Add a sweet, feminine look to a page with beautiful patterned paper.

PARADISE PIER

Denise Pauley
+3: patterned paper,
brads, stitching

Cut photographs into a montage to piece together the memories of an event.

SPRING FLING

Shelley Laming
+3: patterned paper,
stickers, stamps

Don't be afraid to trim letter stickers to make them fit the space on your layout.

Denise Pauley
+3: stickers, stone letters, word tile

Experiment with mixing different fonts on your layouts.

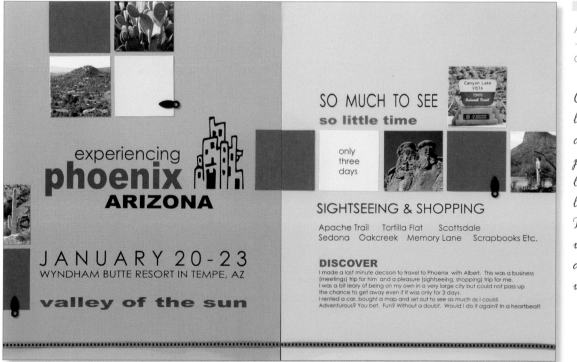

Angie Cramer
+3: photo turns, ribbon, computer font

Check your font collections for interesting dingbats to use as page accents (the building on this layout is part of the Tequila Hill font, which Angie downloaded from www.dafont.com).

TAMALES

As I have watched the health of Guelito and Guelita decline I decided that it was time for me to truly learn the art of Mexican cooking. The recipes of the food we love. Of course learning from Guelita can be challenging because she does not measure the ingredients in the conventional way. She uses her hands to measure and knows from the texture what is missing and how much to add. There is no written recipe.

The basic tamales recipe includes the maza mixture with baking powder, chile and water. Then comes the filling. Traditionally she makes a pork filling but the children prefer beans.

TAMALES

Allison Kimball

+3: patterned paper, stitching, computer font (title)

Stitch "homes" for your photographs, journaling and page accents.

to stories of their lives, cooking tips & even some jokes were shared as we mixed masa, spread it on the corn husks & filled the individual tamales.

I watched as the old wrinkled hands perfectly move in rhythm with the tasks. I felt like I was intruding on a choreographed dance that has been performed throughout the ages. I don't know if I will ever cook like my grandmother but I will be able to pass down the traditions of my family to my children & maybe someday move in the rhythm with my predecessors.

April 28, 2004

Tamales are traditionally made at Christmas time throughout Mexico & they are always a favorite at Guelita's home. Thankfully for us, Guelita makes them occasionally during the year.

Tamales are not difficult to make, but they do take considerable time, so we relish the occasions when we get to eat them (even if I forget how to spell occasion :))

I loved my official cooking lessons with Guelito & Guelita & have many more to look forward

FRIENDS

Lisa Brown Caveney
+3: patterned paper, foam
stamps, computer fonts

Feature more photographs on your page by cutting them into one shape and size.

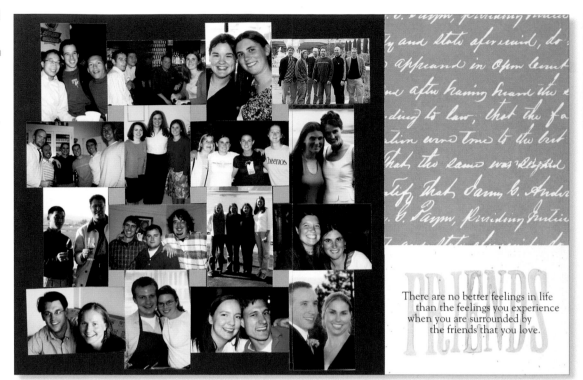

There are no better feelings in life
than the feelings you experience
when you are surrounded by
the friends that you love.

MY DRESS

Lisa Brown Caveney
+3: fabric scraps, chip-
board frame, metal letters

*Embellish a layout
with scraps of silk
and brocade.*

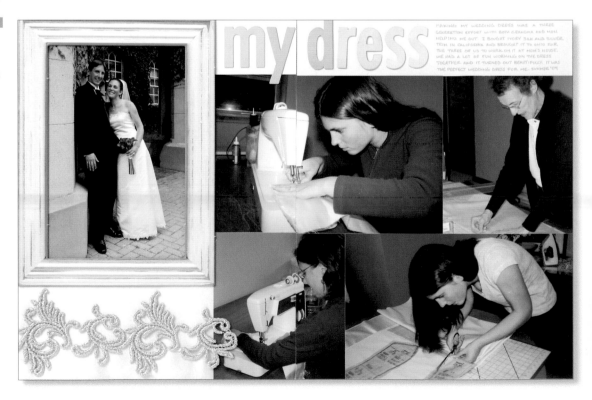

7 THINGS TO TRY
FROM THIS CHAPTER

As a scrapbooker, I'm always excited to try something new on my pages. Here are seven assignments that will allow you to play with the ideas I presented in this chapter:

1. Cut page elements into rectangles and layer them on your page horizontally, as Angie Cramer did on her "The Magic of Christmas" layout (page 113).

2. Use a square punch to create a tiled border or page background.

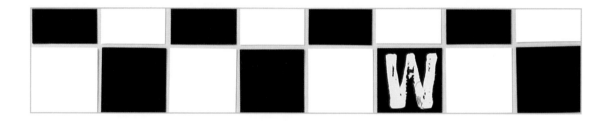

3. Make photocopies of official documents and use them as page embellishments.

4. Tie ribbons onto a page frame, like I did on my "Christmas 2004" layout (page 103).

5. Add personal memorabilia, such as silk, ribbon and lace from a favorite dress or project, to your layout.

6. Create your own photo mosaic, like Denise Pauley did on her "Paradise Pier" layout (page 116).

7. Use the names of the people in your photographs as a clever page border.

LONDON

Lisa Brown Caveney
+3: patterned paper, plastic washer, twine

Crop all of your photographs to the same height (here, 2¾″) and tile them in the middle of your layout.

LONDON

THE TUBE • LONDON BRIDGE • TELEPHONE BOOTH • BEEFEATER • PARLIAMENT • DOUBLE DECKER BUS • HORSE GUARD • BIG BEN

MINI
BOOK

At my bridal shower, my bridesmaids had each of the guests write me something
on a note card. I wanted to incorporate the notes into a mini album, so I bought
envelopes slightly larger than the cards. I bound the envelopes together by punch-
ing holes in them and tying them with a ribbon. I put a photo from the event on
the front of each envelope with the guest's name on the back, and then tucked her
corresponding note card into that section.

6.5.04 BRIDAL SHOWER

Lisa Brown Caveney
+3: stickers, memorabilia (personalized notes), ribbon

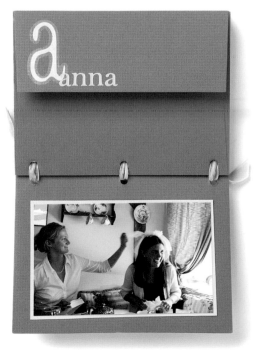

TAKE ANOTHER LOOK ...
AT THESE LETTERING OPTIONS

Why do we scrapbook? It's most often to share a story about our pictures, to creatively preserve the memories of our lives. I love that there are so many lettering options available for scrapbookers to help us do just that. Here's a look back at several of my favorites from this chapter:

MY DRESS
Lisa Brown Caveney
Lettering: metal letters
Effect: brings the reader's eye to the silver brocade trim on Lisa's dress

ROTHENBURG
Lisa Brown Caveney
Lettering: fabric letters
Effect: sets the mood for the rustic and charming city

ALHAMBRA
Lisa Brown Caveney
Lettering: foam stamps with white acrylic paint
Effect: draws attention to the focal-point photograph

CROSSWORD
Lisa Brown Caveney
Lettering: rub-ons
Effect: creates a clever title that ties in with the page theme

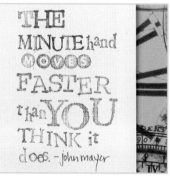

THE MINUTE HAND
Denise Pauley
Lettering: rubber stamps with black ink
Effect: adds a poignant and thoughtful look to the concept of passing time

EXPERIENCEING PHOENIX, ARIZONA
Angie Cramer
Lettering: computer font
Effect: adds a clean and graphic feel to the layout

SKY'S
THE LIMIT

Chapter Five

In this chapter, the sky's the limit! Here, we'll teach you how to create beautiful scrapbook pages with four and more embellishments on each layout.

the possibilities are limitless

AS DEREK AND I SET OFF ON OUR LIVES TOGETHER I WONDER WHAT THE FUTURE HAS IN STORE FOR US. WILL WE STAY IN CALIFORNIA OR WILL WE MOVE SOMEWHERE ELSE? WHERE WILL WE BUY A HOUSE AND WHAT WILL IT LOOK LIKE? HOW MANY CHILDREN WILL WE HAVE? HOW MANY GRANDKIDS? HOW WILL WE CELEBRATE OUR ONE YEAR ANNIVERSARY? WHAT ABOUT OUR TENTH, OUR TWENTY-FIFTH, OR OUR FIFTIETH? THERE ARE SO MANY PATHS THAT OUR LIVES COULD TAKE. I KNOW THAT MY FUTURE LIES WITH DEREK BUT OTHER THAN THAT THE POSSIBILITIES ARE LIMITLESS. WHATEVER HAPPENS WE WILL HAVE EACH OTHER AND I LOOK FORWARD TO DISCOVERING WHAT OUR FUTURE HOLDS FOR US IN THE COMING YEARS.   JULY 17, 2004

the joys of a good book the joys of a good book

EVER SINCE I LEARNED TO READ I HAVE BEEN HOOKED ON BOOKS.
ARE QUITE VARIED — CLASSICS, HISTORY, MODERN FICTION, PLAYS,
HAS ALWAYS BEEN A GREAT COMFORT TO ME. WHENEVER I AM
LOSING MYSELF IN A BOOK IS USUALLY THE BEST WAY FOR
THINGS ARE I MAKE SURE TO SET ASIDE TIME FOR MYSELF
TO READ IS IN BED BEFORE I GO TO SLEEP. I LIKE TO FALL
AMAZED BY THE JOYS OF A GOOD BOOK. IT PROVIDES ME MY

GOOD BOOK

Lisa Brown Caveney

+4: patterned paper, chain, library cards, rub-ons

Record a list of restaurants visited, books read, movies watched or plays seen throughout the last year on a layout.

Book spines (left to right):

- Arthur Koestler — Darkness at Noon
- THE KEYS OF EGYPT — LESLEY AND ROY ADKINS — Harper Collins
- ARTHUR MILLER / AFTER THE FALL
- AUSTEN — PERSUASION — OXFORD
- VOLTAIRE ◆ Candide — Penguin
- ROSS KING — Brunelleschi's Dome — Penguin
- NICK HORNBY — HOW TO BE GOOD
- DELL FIC — GOD BLESS YOU, MR. ROSEWATER — KURT VONNEGUT, JR.
- THE LOVELY BONES — ALICE SEBOLD
- Collected Works of Oscar Wilde

I SIMPLY LOVE TO READ. MY INTERESTS
SCIENCE - I LOVE IT ALL. READING
STRESSED OUT, FRUSTRATED, OR DEPRESSED
ME TO RELAX. NO MATTER HOW BUSY
TO READ EVERYDAY. MY FAVORITE TIME
ASLEEP READING. I AM CONSTANTLY
PERSONAL RETREAT TO REFRESH AND INSPIRE ME.

2004

THE MYSTERIES BY ROBERT McGILL

THE GOOD EARTH BY PEARL S. BUCK

THE SECRET LIFE OF BEES BY SUE
  MONK KIDD

THE SILMARILLION BY J.R.R TOLKIEN

IN THE WAKE OF THE PLAGUE: THE
  BLACK DEATH AND THE WORLD IT
  MADE BY N.F. CANTOR

CAT'S EYE BY MARGARET ATWOOD

THE GUTENBERG REVOLUTION BY JOHN MAN

BRO DART   CAT No. 23-104   PRINTED IN U.S.A

FAMILY BIKE RIDE

Lisa Brown Caveney
+4: patterned paper,
hinges, ink, metal
embellishments

*Combine ink and
metal for an active,
outdoor look*

ARDENWOOD FARM PUMPKINS

Lisa Brown Caveney
+5: patterned paper,
label holder, paint,
ribbon, stickers

*Use colorful
patterned paper to
set the mood for a
seasonal layout*

Lisa Brown Caveney
+4: patterned paper,
photo corners, staples,
stickers

*Use photo corners
or create your own
to give your photos
a finished look*

STANDING THIRTY-THREE METERS IN HEIGHT
THE MAIN TEMPLE AT LAMANAI IS ONE OF THE
LARGEST PRECLASSICAL STRUCTURES IN THE
MAYA AREA. THE INITIAL PHASE CONSTRUCTION
BEGAN IN 100 B.C. AND IT WAS ABANDONED
IN THE EARLY POSTCLASSIC PERIOD. DEREK AND
I CLIMBED THE STEEP STEPS TO THE TOP
OF THE TEMPLE AND WERE REWARDED WITH
A STUNNING VIEW. WE COULD SEE THE NEW
RIVER AND LOOK OVER THE TOP OF THE
JUNGLE CANOPY FOR MILES. 11-24-04

lamanai

2 OCEANS

Lisa Brown Caveney
+5: fabric, metal
embellishments, molding,
paint, stickers

*Give your page
textural appeal by
adding fabric,
raised molding
and dimensional
embellishments.*

ON OUR SECOND DAY IN CAPE TOWN
DEREK AND I DROVE OUT TO THE CAPE OF
GOOD HOPE NATURE RESERVE. IT WAS
AN OVERCAST DAY WITH ON AND OFF RAIN
BUT WE MADE THE BEST OF IT AND
ENJOYED OUR TRIP IMMENSELY. WE PARKED
THE CAR AND WALKED OUT TO CAPE
POINT. THE VIEWS ALONG OUR WALK
WERE SPECTACULAR. THE OCEAN WAS
A BRILLIANT TEAL AND CONTRASTED WITH
GRASS COVERED CLIFFS THAT WERE
BRIGHT GREEN FROM ALL THE WINTER
RAIN. THE CLIFFS WERE ROUGH AND
SEEMED TO SPROUT FROM THE OCEAN.
THE WAVES POUNDED FEROCIOUSLY AT
THE SHORE PRODUCING QUITE AN EFFECT.
WHEN WE GOT TO THE LOOKOUT AT
THE END OF THE WALK IT SEEMED
THAT THE OCEANS WENT ON FOREVER. IT
WAS NEAT TO BE STANDING AT THE
SPOT WHERE THE INDIAN AND
ATLANTIC OCEANS MEET.
AUGUST 4, 2004

2 oceans

CARLA'S SHOWER

Lisa Brown Caveney
+4: patterned paper,
metal embellishments,
ribbon, rub-ons

*Maximize your
space by creating
a tile pattern with
your photos.*

BAS SHOWER

Lisa Brown Caveney
+5: patterned paper,
buttons, faux flowers,
stickers, vellum

*Add a twist to your
layout by adding
tinted vellum to a
photo.*

9 TIPS FOR **WELL-DESIGNED SCRAPBOOK PAGES**

When I create a scrapbook page, I always design with a purpose in mind. It's important to have a visual goal of what you want to achieve with your layout before you start selecting paper and embellishments. Here are a few of my favorite page design tips:

1. Don't include anything that doesn't contribute to the message of your layout. Avoid adding for the sake of adding.

2. Keep a consistent tone throughout all design elements; they should work together to communicate a unified message.

3. Use your layout design to reinforce your photos by taking into account the level of action, and the color and the presence of your photos. Mimic color schemes found in your photos, choose colors that suit the mood of the layout, or use shapes found in your photos to create greater harmony and continuity.

4. Lines within a layout are a natural way to draw focus. Horizontal lines create a calm feeling while vertical lines create a feeling of movement. Curves are also powerful design elements.

5. Try not to trap interior space. Concentrating negative space on the outside edges of a layout helps pull the focus into the center instead of off the page.

6. Design across the page break on two-page layouts. Spanning pictures and elements across both pages unifies the layout; however, be sure to avoid cutting through someone's head or another critical element.

7. Concentrate heavier elements on the bottom of the page to provide balance.

8. Remember that white space can be a simple but powerful design element.

9. Use the rule of thirds: divide your layout into a tic-tac-toe grid. The locations where the lines in the grid cross are natural human focal points.

Happy Holidays from Oakland, California! We hope this letter finds you and your family happy and healthy. 2004 has been a good year for us. As Derek put it, "We got married, I finished my PhD, and the Calgary Flames went to the Stanley Cup. What could be better?"

The highlight of the year for us was our wedding in London, Ontario on July 17, 2004. After many months of planning and preparation, we had a beautiful wedding day. Everything was perfect, despite some ominous clouds and a bit of rain cutting our cocktail hour a few minutes short. It was a wonderful day surrounded by our dear friends and family and we couldn't have asked for more. The following morning Derek's parents kept the festivities going by hosting a brunch at their house and we enjoyed the extra time to spend with everyone who made the journey to our wedding.

For our honeymoon we headed off to South Africa for three weeks with a few day stop in Amsterdam on the way home. Derek's parents hosted a wedding brunch for us with Derek's South African relatives. It was a great way for Lisa to meet the family and we had a wonderful time chatting and enjoying good food. During our stay in South Africa we packed in a lot. We visited relatives, went hiking in the Drakensberg Mountains, experienced the charm of Cullinan, spotted amazing wildlife in Kruger National Park, went curio shopping at Hartebeespoort Dam, enjoyed the beauty of Cape Town, hiked around Cape Point, went wine tasting in Stellenbosch, and toured Pretoria. It was an amazing trip and we want to extend a hearty thank you to all of Derek's relatives who showed us such hospitality during our time in their beautiful country.

We were able to reciprocate a bit of the South African generosity when a business trip brought Derek's uncle, Phil, to California. Unfortunately Derek was in Germany at the time, but Lisa had fun playing tour guide in Derek's absence with Lisa, Phil, and Phil's coworker going everywhere from Fort Point to Muir Woods.

2004 marked the culmination of five years of Derek's hard work when he graduated with his PhD from Berkeley in May. Derek's parents flew out to California for the special occasion and we enjoyed the commencement ceremony at Hearst Greek Theatre, especially when Dr. Hedrick hooded Derek. The rest of the weekend was spent enjoying graduation parties while Derek was settling in to his new title. Derek's parents stayed with us for a week and enjoyed a trip to Yosemite with Derek before heading back home to London.

Following graduation, Derek spent some time in London with his parents and took a fun trip with his dad out to his parent's new property in Elgin County. While Derek was in London he also had his bachelor party and spent the weekend with his friends golfing, playing paint ball, and a doing a few other nameless bachelor party activities. Meanwhile back in California, Lisa's girlfriends were throwing her a wedding

JANUARY   APRIL   MAY

CHRISTMAS LETTER 2004

Lisa Brown Caveney
+4: computer font, rub-ons, stickers, twill

Save time by using your Christmas newsletter as journaling to recap the events of the past year.

shower and bachelorette party. Lisa's bridesmaids hosted an afternoon tea for the wedding shower and they spent the rest of the weekend sightseeing in San Francisco and wine tasting in Napa Valley.

We both celebrated our five year college reunions this year. In April, Lisa headed back to Durham, North Carolina for her Duke University reunion. She had a fabulous time getting together with her girl friends, going out to dinner with her engineering buddies, and catching up with former professors. In October, Lisa joined Derek in heading to Kingston, Ontario for Derek's reunion at Queen's University. We had fun checking out Derek's old haunts with his university friends and of course we attended ritual on Friday afternoon. The weekend was also homecoming for Queen's and we enjoyed watching the Golden Gaels take on the Mustangs, but unfortunately Western routed Queen's.

2004 has been a year of travel for us. In addition to Lisa's numerous business trips and Derek's two visits to Munich to wrap up his collaboration with BMW, we had a number of fun trips this year. Over the course of the spring and early summer, we had a number of wedding planning trips to London and Lisa went to Cleveland twice to work on her wedding dress and the wedding cake with her mother and grandmother with a little side time for bicycle rides with her dad. In February Lisa visited Sarah, Susan, and Stephen in Washington, D.C while Derek went to Zack's bachelor party in Baltimore. In April, Lisa went to Wisconsin for a get together of the creative team of scrapbooking website she works for, Two Peas in a Bucket. April also brought a delightful journey to St. Simons Island, Georgia where we attended Zack and Sarah's wedding. The ceremony was beautiful and we also enjoyed the charm of the island and the beautiful beach. In June, Lisa headed to County Galway in Ireland to attend Erin and Andy's wedding and had a splendid time living in the Irish castle where the wedding was held for the weekend. For the week preceding the wedding, Lisa did a bit of touring and visited some wonderful sights in Belgium and Ireland. In September, we headed to Arizona for a long weekend. After being blessed with good weather for our hike at the Grand Canyon, we were treated to downpours for the rest of our trip as we stopped at Sunset Crater, Wupatki, and Montezuma's Castle. We decided to go on our first cruise over the American Thanksgiving holiday. During the course of the week we went swimming with sting rays in the Cayman Islands, took a zip line canopy tour in the Bay Islands of Honduras, went on a riverboat ride to the Lamanai Mayan ruins in Belize, and biked and snorkeled in Cozumel.

As we bring this letter to a close, we wish you a merry holiday season full of happiness and a joyous new year. All the best,

Lisa and Derek

CHRISTMAS letter 04

SEPTEMBER

NOVEMBER

DECEMBER

DESIGNERS' SECRETS ...
ON FINISHING PAGES

How do you decide when you've added enough embellishments to your page? It can be a challenge to create the right balance. On one hand, you want just enough accents to add personality and charm to your page but not so many that your photographs and journaling are overshadowed. I asked the contributing designers in this book to share their secrets on knowing when a page is finished. Here's what they said:

Q: *How do you know when your page is finished? How do you know when to stop adding page embellishments?*

A. "There is a visual awareness that tells me when I've crossed the line from 'this is good' to 'this is too much.' The page should feel balanced and uncluttered, and most importantly, the photos should always be the stars of the show. The embellishments should support the photos without overwhelming them. Each item placed on a page should feel like it belongs and is there for a reason." —Angie Cramer

A. "I like to use embellishments that will help tell the story. I always use them in odd numbers, such as one or three. I tend to use one embellishment for a focal point and three to create a visual triangle. When I've met those criteria, I stop. Truly ... I just stop when it feels good and done." —Allison Kimball

A. "A completed page has a sense of charm and delight without feeling overdone." —Shelley Laming

A. "Though I'm still not sure when a page is "finished," I do know it's not when I look at it and sense something—anything—is missing. It could be as simple as a touch of ink or different journaling, but sometimes it's so oddly composed it requires a complete makeover. I'm learning that I feel satisfied with a layout when I look at it and know that it effectively tells the story I set out to tell. Maybe it could use a little more of this or that, but if it takes me back in time, I'm happy." —Denise Pauley

Allison Kimball
+5: patterned paper,
chipboard accent, ink,
rub-ons, stamps

When using multiple sheets of patterned paper, maintain the mood of your layout by keeping colors and themes similar.

Angie Cramer
+7: patterned paper,
computer font, metal
embellishments, ribbon,
slide mounts, snap,
tile letters

Take the same challenge as Angie and try capturing a self-portrait without being present.

FAVORITE COLORS

Denise Pauley

+8: patterned paper, bookplate, brads, envelope, ink, paint, stamps, word tabs

Develop a layout based on items that represent you and your loved ones.

Angie Cramer
+4: brads, computer fonts, pebbles, faux flower

Journal specific steps involved with a favorite activity to provide greater detail about a much-loved tradition.

Allison Kimball
+8: patterned paper, chipboard accent, frame, glaze, ink, rub-ons, stamps, template

Use your paper scraps with lettering templates to create words for your title.

REMEMBER

"one of your favorite songs is "He gives flowers to everyone" by cheri call. I appreciate the message this song gives you, in a simple way she is expressing the worth of all

Girls your father and I love you so dearly. Each of you has unique qualities and characteristics that bring such happiness and harmony to our lives. We don't know what the future will hold for you individually. Trials will come and great joy can be found. We hope that you will always remember that we will always be there for you. More important is the knowledge that the Lord loves you and will always be there for you. I love you.
mommy   september 2, 2002

APR 1 8 2005

FLOWERS FOR EVERYONE

Allison Kimball

+7: patterned paper, ink, rub-ons, stamps, tabs, trim, stitching

Look for timesavers, like this cardstock print that Allison pieced, inked and put back together.

people, that Heavenly Father does not value one person over another. He loves us all. He blesses us despite our weaknesses & most especially through our faithfulness.

everyone flowers for

YAKITY YAK

Denise Pauley
+6: patterned paper, chalk, fabric, ink, staples, stickers

Convey a busy mood by incorporating words and numbers onto your layout.

BASKETBALL 2004-05

Angie Cramer
+5: brads, computer fonts, letter tiles, photo turns, word blocks

Convert photos to black and white to mask poor lighting, as Angie did with these photos shot in a gym.

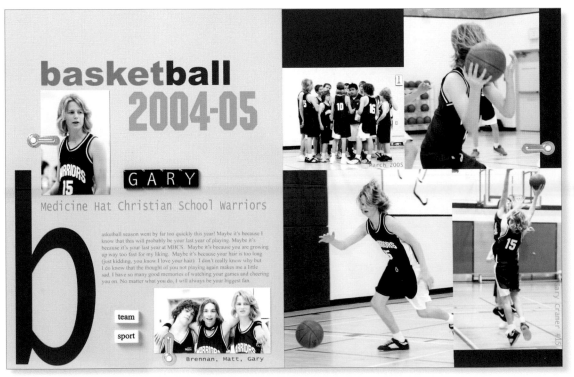

In handwriting on the layout:

Ask yourself if what you're doing today is getting you closer to where you want to be tomorrow. FC Words to Live By

ASK YOURSELF

Shelley Laming

+4: patterned paper, brads, ink, punch

Create your own unique accents with patterned paper, a punch and distressing ink.

THROUGH EVERY AGE

Shelley Laming
+8: ribbon, twill, brad,
twist ties, stickers, ink,
paper flower, stamps

*Place photo corners
on the bottom corners
of your photograph
or photo space to
visually anchor the
images on your page.*

PEDICURES AT SUKI

Lisa Brown Caveney
+4: patterned paper,
chipboard letters, paint,
rub-ons

*Establish a greater
presence on your
page by using
oversized chipboard
lettering and paint.*

THE WORLD IS BUT A CANVAS Thoreau
TO THE IMAGINATION.

ERIN IN SPRING

Denise Pauley

+9: chalk, envelope, eyelets, fabric, hinges, ink,
stamps, sticker, tab

Create a soft look by using chalk ink to stamp your letters.

MINI
BOOK

I have tons of travel photos. I know I'll never be able to scrapbook all of them, so I made this mini album to capture the key moments and memories from each destination. To create it, I cut a 5″ x 5″ square of chipboard for each country or territory I visited and painted each one with white acrylic paint. I attached a photo to the front of each square and listed the name of the country along with some of my favorite memories of the location on the back. I also included some patterned paper on the back of each card to add color and depth to an otherwise simple design. By threading the cards onto a metal chain, I can easily add more cards as I travel to new places.

TRAVEL MINI ALBUM
Lisa Brown Caveney
+5: patterned paper, rub-ons, acrylic paint, metal chain, chipboard

Riverboat Ride on
the New River
Mayan Temples at
Lamanai
Howler Monkeys
Belikin Beer
Looking over the top
of the jungle canopy
Beautiful wood
carvings

Belize

Windmills
Rijksmuseum
Wooden Shoes
Anne Frank House
Lovely Tulips
bicycles everywhere
Van Gogh Museum
Rembrandt House
Museum

Netherlands

MINI
BOOK

Versailles
eating crepes
The Louvre
blue waters of Nice
Chateaux of the Loire Valley
Eiffel Tower
L'Arc de Triomphe
Musee D'orsay
The Metro
Notre Dame
Sacre Coeur

France

Dingle Peninsula
Bike Ride
Sheep
Cliffs of Moher
Doors of Dublin
Book of Kells
Pub Food
Guiness Brewery
Kilmainham Jail

Ireland

Uffizi Gallery
The David
Hiking in Cinque Terre
Gelato
Canals of Venice
Coliseum + Forum
Glass Museum in
     Murano
Leaning Tower of Pisa
The Duomo

Italy

Where I am from
Continental states
Plus Hawaii
Amazing National Park
     System
Road Trips
Diverse eco Systems
Rocky Mountains
Grand Canyon

USA

M&L

Lisa Brown Caveney
+4: patterned paper,
eyelets, ribbon, stickers

Create a lattice pattern with a variety of textured ribbons or cardstock. Keep the layout simple to offset the complexity of the pattern.

HALL OF MIRRORS

Lisa Brown Caveney
+4: patterned paper,
mirrors, ribbon, rub-ons

For greater continuity, incorporate elements into your page design that reflect the subject or location of your layout.

Lisa Brown Caveney
+4: patterned paper,
clips, stickers, ribbon

*Make a layout
about favorite col-
ors, clothes, books,
food, etc.—it's a
great way to record
insights about you
or loved ones.*

Lisa Brown Caveney
+5: patterned paper,
computer font, quote,
ribbon, stickers

*Commemorate special
relationships by
pulling in design ele-
ments to reflect your
loved one's personality.*

Neighborhood Inspiration Walk

When I need to find inspiration
for a page design, one of my
favorite things to do is to walk
around my neighborhood.
This tiled floor inspired my title
design—I cut irregularly
shaped diamonds from cardstock and placed a letter on
each one. Try this exercise for
yourself to see what inspiration you can find in your
neighborhood!

6 THINGS TO TRY
FROM THIS CHAPTER

I'm always looking for ways to add depth and creativity to my pages. Here are a few ideas gathered from this chapter that may help you reach a new level of creativity:

1. Create your own unique statement about what a completed page includes and try to stick to it throughout your creative process.

2. If you're limited to one or two photos from an event, challenge yourself to use them to their fullest capacity (see "BAS Shower" on page 132).

3. Play with lines. Analyze how vertical, horizontal and curved lines impact your layout.

4. Use color as a unique way to represent different personalities, similar to the method used in Denise Pauley's "Favorite Colors" layout on page 138.

5. Consider your daily routine and create a layout that focuses on one specific habit, like Angie Cramer did in "Sleep" on page 137.

6. Take note of logos and other patterns found at restaurants, retailers and grocery stores and use one that catches your eye as inspiration for a page.

TAKE ANOTHER LOOK ... AT PATTERNED PAPER AS A DESIGN ELEMENT

Patterned papers have made a comeback! No longer used simply for background paper, they're perfect for creating page embellishments or other strong design elements. Here's a second look at the creative ways we used patterned paper in this chapter:

I USED TO BE
Allison Kimball

Application: large, isolated shapes cut with scissors

Impact: an easy and inexpensive embellishment

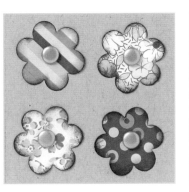

ASK
Shelley Laming

Application: shapes cut with a paper punch from a variety of patterns

Impact: a simple and varied design pattern

CARLA'S SHOWER
Lisa Brown Caveney

Application: a photo mat

Impact: a fun, fresh look

M&L
Lisa Brown Caveney

Application: a border

Impact: clean and simple

FLOWERS FOR EVERYONE
Allison Kimball

Application: separation between photos

Impact: fun and energetic

YAKITY YAKITY YAK
Denise Pauley

Application: a round design element

Impact: sets the busy mood Denise is trying to convey

SUPPLY LISTS

Chapter 1

10-11 | HANAUMA BAY

LISA BROWN CAVENEY

Supplies *Textured cardstock:* Bazzill Basics Paper; *Pens:* Zig Writer, EK Success; Gelly Roll, Sakura.

12 | BAOBAB

LISA BROWN CAVENEY

Supplies *Textured cardstock:* Bazzill Basics Paper; *Pen:* Gelly Roll, Sakura.

12 | FLIGHT

LISA BROWN CAVENEY

Supplies *Textured cardstock:* Bazzill Basics Paper; *Pen:* Zig Writer, EK Success.

13 | TUGELA GORGE HIKE

LISA BROWN CAVENEY

Supplies *Textured cardstock:* Bazzill Basics Paper; *Pens:* Zig Writer, EK Success; Gelly Roll, Sakura.

13 | MUIR WOODS

LISA BROWN CAVENEY

Supplies *Textured cardstock:* Bazzill Basics Paper; *Circle punch:* Marvy Uchida; *Pen:* Zig Writer, EK Success.

14 | HONU

LISA BROWN CAVENEY

Supplies *Textured cardstock:* Bazzill Basics Paper; *Pen:* Zig Writer, EK Success.

14 | OLD, NEW, BORROWED, BLUE

LISA BROWN CAVENEY

Supplies *Textured cardstock:* Bazzill Basics Paper; *Pen:* Zig Writer, EK Success.

16 | CANADIAN THANKSGIVING

LISA BROWN CAVENEY

Supplies *Textured cardstock:* Bazzill Basics Paper; *Pen:* Zig Writer, EK Success.

16 | SOUTH AFRICAN FAMILY

LISA BROWN CAVENEY

Supplies *Textured cardstock:* Bazzill Basics Paper; *Pen:* Zig Writer, EK Success

17 | ZACK & SARAH'S WEDDING

LISA BROWN CAVENEY

Supplies *Textured cardstock:* Bazzill Basics Paper; *Corner rounder and circle punch:* Marvy Uchida; *Pen:* Zig Writer, EK Success.

17 | GEAR

LISA BROWN CAVENEY

Supplies *Textured cardstock:* Bazzill Basics Paper; *Pen:* Zig Writer, EK Success.

18-19 | OCTOBER

LISA BROWN CAVENEY

Supplies *Textured cardstock:* Bazzill Basics Paper; *Circle punch:* Marvy Uchida; *Pen:* Gelly Roll, Sakura.

21 | DECK OF CARDS

DENISE PAULEY

Supplies *Textured cardstock:* Paper Adventures, Canson and Pebbles Inc.; *Lettering template:* Type, ScrapPagerz; *Rectangle punch:* Paper Shapers, EK Success; *Crimper:* Fiskars; *Pen:* Pigment Pro, American Crafts.

21 | RANDOM ADVICE #105

SHELLEY LAMING

Supplies *Textured cardstock:* Bazzill Basics Paper; *Pen:* Zig Writer, EK Success; *Markers:* Crayola.

22-23 | SILLY

ALLISON KIMBALL

PHOTOS BY JESSI STRINGHAM PHOTOGRAPHY

Supplies *Textured cardstock:* Bazzill Basics Paper and source unknown; *Pen:* Gelly Roll, Sakura; *Other:* X-acto knife.

24 | ERIN'S EYES

DENISE PAULEY

Supplies *Cardstock:* Making Memories and Paper Adventures; *Pen:* Pigment Pro, American Crafts; *Flower:* Denise's own design.

25 | CASSIDY & CHANDLER

SHELLEY LAMING

Supplies *Textured cardstock:* Bazzill Basics Paper; *Pen:* Zig Writer, EK Success.

26 | AN UNEXPECTED HAPPY

DENISE PAULEY

Supplies *Cardstock:* Pebbles Inc. and American Crafts; *Pen:* Pigment Pro, American Crafts.

26 | BABOONS

LISA BROWN CAVENEY

Supplies *Textured cardstock:* Bazzill Basics Paper; *Pen:* Zig Writer, EK Success.

27 | HEAVEN/EARTH

ANGIE CRAMER

Supplies *Cardstock:* Bazzill Basics Paper.

27 | I LOVE ...

SHELLEY LAMING

Supplies *Textured cardstock:* Bazzill Basics Paper; *Pen:* Zig Writer, EK Success.

72 | CHICAGO

DENISE PAULEY

Supplies *Textured cardstock:* Bazzill Basics Paper; *Brads:* Making Memories; *Computer font:* Cornerstone and Garamond, Microsoft Word.

74-75 | CROSS COUNTRY

LISA BROWN CAVENEY

Supplies *Textured cardstock:* Bazzill Basics Paper; *Letter stickers:* Sticker Studio; *Metal letters:* Making Memories; *Pen:* Zig Writer, EK Success.

77 | DADDY & SARAH

SHELLEY LAMING

Supplies *Textured cardstock:* Bazzill Basics Paper; *Pen:* Zig Writer, EK Success; *Other:* Fabric.

77 | ATTACK

ALLISON KIMBALL

Supplies *Textured cardstock:* Chatterbox, Bazzill Basics Paper and source unknown; *Patterned paper:* Chatterbox; *Pens:* Gelly Roll, Sakura; Zig Writer, EK Success; *Computer font:* Times New Roman, Microsoft Word; *Other:* Thread and X-acto knife.

78-79 | SIX

ALLISON KIMBALL

Supplies *Textured cardstock:* Bazzill Basics Paper and source unknown; *Patterned paper:* American Crafts; *Pens:* Gelly Roll, Sakura; Zig Writer, EK Success; *Brads:* Karen Foster Design and Provo Craft; *Other:* X-acto knife.

80 | TWEENDOM

SHELLEY LAMING

Supplies *Textured cardstock:* Bazzill Basics Paper; *Letter stickers:* Doodlebug Designs; *Stamping ink:* ColorBox, Clearsnap; *Pen:* Zig Writer, EK Success.

80 | SUGAR & SPICE

ALLISON KIMBALL

Supplies *Textured cardstock, patterned paper and letter stickers:* Chatterbox; *Pens:* Pigment Pro, American Crafts; Zig Writer, EK Success.

81 | LET'S DANCE

ANGIE CRAMER

Supplies *Computer font:* Times New Roman, Microsoft Word; *Other:* Ribbon.

81 | ALL GIRL

ANGIE CRAMER

Supplies *Printed transparency:* Art Warehouse, Creative Imaginations; *Brads:* Provo Craft.

82 | INSPEARATIONS

DENISE PAULEY

Supplies *Textured cardstock:* Impress Rubber Stamps, Making Memories and Pebbles Inc.; *Foam stamps:* Making Memories; *Acrylic paint:* Delta Technical Coatings; *Pen:* Zig Millennium, EK Success.

83 | HAPPY NINETEENTH BIRTHDAY

ANGIE CRAMER

Supplies *Patterned paper:* KI Memories and Fiddlerz 3; *Computer font:* Arial Narrow, Microsoft Word.

83 | ONE MOMENT

ALLISON KIMBALL

Supplies *Textured cardstock:* Bazzill Basics Paper; *Patterned paper:* KI Memories; *Chipboard letters:* Li'l Davis Designs; *Pen:* Gel Xtreme, Yasutomo.

84 | CHRISTMAS CARD

ALLISON KIMBALL

Supplies *Patterned paper:* Rhonna Farrer for Autumn Leaves; *Pen:* Gelly Roll, Sakura; *Other:* Christmas card.

85 | PLAY, SCORE, COUNT

DENISE PAULEY

Supplies *Patterned paper:* Keeping Memories Alive; *Letter stamps:* PSX Design; *Square stamps:* Technique Tuesday; *Stamping ink:* Fluid Chalk, ColorBox, Clearsnap; *Pen:* Staedtler.

86-87 | ITALY

LISA BROWN CAVENEY

Supplies *Letter stamps:* PSX Design; *Stamping ink:* Stampin' Up!; *Other:* Map wrapping paper and lettering template.

88 | I LOVE TO WRITE

DENISE PAULEY

Supplies *Textured cardstock:* Bazzill Basics Paper; *Patterned paper:* BasicGrey; *Pen:* Pigment Pro, American Crafts; *Other:* Stitching.

89 | FUN & GAMES

ANGIE CRAMER

Supplies *Digital patterned paper:* ShabbyPrincess.com; *Computer fonts:* Russell Square (title), downloaded from www.1001fonts.com; Verdana (journaling), downloaded from www.myfonts.com.

89 | CARLY, ABBY & CHANDLER

SHELLEY LAMING

Supplies *Textured cardstock:* Bazzill Basics Paper; *Stamping ink:* ColorBox, Clearsnap; *Greeting card:* Marcel Shurman for American Greetings; *Pen:* Zig Writer, EK Success.

90 | WALTER BROWN, JR.

LISA BROWN CAVENEY

Supplies *Twill tape:* Scenic Route Paper Co.; *Pen:* Gelly Roll, Sakura; *Other:* Vintage wrapping paper.

91 | DEREK

LISA BROWN CAVENEY

Supplies *Album:* Kolo; *Letter rub-ons and metal tag:* Making Memories; *Graphic rub-ons:* KI Memories.

116 | PARADISE PIER

DENISE PAULEY

Supplies *Textured cardstock:* DieCuts with a View (blue and white) Bazzill Basics Paper (green), and American Crafts (yellow); *Patterned paper:* DieCuts with a View; *Brads:* Impress Rubber Stamps; *Pen:* Pigment Pro, American Crafts.

116 | SPRING FLING

SHELLEY LAMING

Supplies *Textured cardstock:* Bazzill Basics Paper; *Patterned paper:* Scrapworks; *Letter stickers:* Wordsworth; *Letter stamps:* PSX Design; *Pen:* Zig Writer, EK Success.

117 | RYAN ON EASTER

DENISE PAULEY

Supplies *Textured cardstock:* Bazzill Basics Paper (green and orange), Arctic Frog (blue); *Letter stickers:* Creative Memories; *Stone letters:* EK Success; *"Memories" tile:* Making Memories; *Pen:* Pigment Pro, American Crafts.

117 | EXPERIENCING PHOENIX, ARIZONA

ANGIE CRAMER

Supplies *Ribbon and photo turns:* Making Memories; *Computer fonts:* Arial Black (titles), Microsoft Word; Century Gothic (some subtitles and journaling) and Tequila Hill (dingbat for building), downloaded from the Internet.

118-119 | TAMALES

ALLISON KIMBALL

Supplies *Textured cardstock:* Chatterbox; *Patterned papers:* Autumn Leaves and Anna Griffin; *Pen:* Pigment Pro, American Crafts; *Computer font:* Times New Roman, Microsoft Word.

120 | FRIENDS

LISA BROWN CAVENEY

Supplies *Patterned paper:* Scenic Route Paper Co.; *Foam stamps:* Making Memories; *Acrylic paint:* Plaid Enterprises; *Quote:* Two Peas in a Bucket; *Computer font:* Goudy Old Style, downloaded from the Internet.

120 | MY DRESS

LISA BROWN CAVENEY

Supplies *Textured cardstock:* Bazzill Basics Paper; *Metal letters:* KI Memories; *Silk:* Silk Road Fabrics; *Silver trim:* Britex Fabrics; *Pen:* Gelly Roll, Sakura; *Other:* Chipboard frame.

122-123 | LONDON

LISA BROWN CAVENEY

Supplies *Patterned paper:* The Paper Loft; *Boshers:* Bazzill Basics Paper; *Twine:* Darice; *Pen:* Zig Writer, EK Success; *Other:* Lettering template.

124 | 6.5.04 BRIDAL SHOWER

LISA BROWN CAVENEY

Supplies *Textured cardstock and envelopes:* Bazzill Basics Paper; *Ribbon:* May Arts; *Letter stickers:* Mustard Moon (white) and Chatterbox (pink); *Pen:* Zig Writer, EK Success.

Chapter 5

128-129 | JOYS OF A GOOD BOOK

LISA BROWN CAVENEY

Supplies *Patterned paper:* 7gypsies; *Rub-ons and metal chain:* Making Memories; *Pen:* Zig Writer, EK Success; *Other:* Library cards.

130 | FAMILY BIKE RIDE

LISA BROWN CAVENEY

Supplies *Patterned paper:* 7gypsies; *Metal letters and hinges:* Making Memories; *Letter stamps:* Ma Vinci's Reliquary (big), Hero Arts (small); *Stamping ink:* Stampin' Up!; *Pen:* Zig Writer, EK Success.

130 | ARDENWOOD FARM PUMPKINS

LISA BROWN CAVENEY

Supplies *Patterned paper:* Scrapbook Wizard; *Letter stickers:* Chatterbox; *Foam stamps, acrylic paint and label holder:* Making Memories; *Pen:* Zig Writer, EK Success; *Other:* Ribbon.

131 | LAMANAI

LISA BROWN CAVENEY

Supplies *Patterned paper:* BasicGrey; *Leather corners:* Making Memories; *Letter stickers:* American Crafts; *Pen:* Gelly Roll, Sakura; *Other:* Staples.

131 | 2 OCEANS

LISA BROWN CAVENEY

Supplies *Textured cardstock:* Bazzill Basics Paper; *Number sticker:* American Crafts; *Metal molding, metal letters and acrylic paint:* Making Memories.

132 | CARLA'S SHOWER

LISA BROWN CAVENEY

Supplies *Patterned paper:* Chatterbox; *Ribbon, ribbon charms and rub-ons:* Making Memories; *Pen:* Zig Writer, EK Success.

132 | BAS SHOWER

LISA BROWN CAVENEY

Supplies *Patterned paper:* KI Memories; *Vellum:* Emagination Crafts; *Letter stickers:* American Crafts (large) and Chatterbox (small); *Paper flowers:* Making Memories; *Buttons:* Hillcreek Designs; *Pen:* Zig Writer, EK Success.

134-135 | CHRISTMAS LETTER 2004

LISA BROWN CAVENEY

Supplies *Textured cardstock:* Bazzill Basics Paper; *Rub-ons:* Making Memories (date postmark), Autumn Leaves (month, "Christmas"); *Twill tape:* Scenic Route Paper Co.; *Letter stickers:* Doodlebug Designs; *Computer font:* Times New Roman, Microsoft Word.

137 | USED TO BE

ALLISON KIMBALL

PHOTO BY JESSI STRINGHAM PHOTOGRAPHY

Supplies *Patterned papers:* BasicGrey and Scenic Route Paper Co.; *Chipboard accent:* Li'l Davis Designs; *Rub-ons:* KI Memories; *Date stamp:* OfficeMax; *Stamping ink:* Stampin' Up! and Clearsnap; *Monogram stamp:* Custom made; *Pen:* Pigment Pro, American Crafts.

137 | SLEEP

ANGIE CRAMER

Supplies *Textured cardstock:* Bazzill Basics Paper; *Patterned paper, floral frame and accents:* Anna Griffin; *Ribbon and black snap:* Making Memories; *Slide mount (colored):* Color Oasis, EK Success; *Tile letters (black):* Paper Bliss; *Computer font:* Times New Roman, Microsoft Word; *Other:* Black slide mounts and metal accents.

138 | FAVORITE COLORS

DENISE PAULEY

Supplies *Textured cardstock:* Bazzill Basics Paper (blue and green), Impress Rubber Stamps (pink), source unknown (beige); *Patterned paper:* Déjà Views by The C-Thru Ruler Co.; *Foam stamps, acrylic paint and envelopes:* Making Memories; *Brads:* Making Memories (silver), K&Company (green); *Letter stamps:* PSX Design; *Stamping ink:* StazOn, Tsukineko; Fluid Chalk, ColorBox, Clearsnap; *Bookplate:* Li'l Davis Designs; *Word tabs:* Autumn Leaves; *Pen:* Pigma Micron, Sakura.

139 | THE ROAD WELL TRAVELED

ANGIE CRAMER

Supplies *Brads and page pebbles:* Making Memories; *Computer fonts:* Times New Roman, Microsoft Word (journaling); Serpentine, downloaded from *www.1001fonts.com* (title), Square 721 BT, downloaded from *www.myfonts.com* ("Summer 2004"); Wingdings 3, Microsoft Word (arrows); and Sundings JL, downloaded from *www.dafont.com; Other:* Silk flower.

139 | BASKETBALL

ALLISON KIMBALL

Supplies *Textured cardstock:* Bazzill Basics Paper and source unknown; *Patterned paper, frame and rub-ons:* Chatterbox; *Chipboard accent:* Li'l Davis Designs; *Lettering template:* ScrapPagerz.com; *Date stamp:* OfficeMax; *Stamping ink:* Stampin' Up! and Clearsnap; *Monogram stamp:* Custom made; *Dimensional glaze:* Diamond Glaze, JudiKins; *Pen:* Pigment Pro, American Crafts.

140-141 | FLOWERS FOR EVERYONE

ALLISON KIMBALL

Supplies *Patterned paper:* Christina Cole for Provo Craft; *Tab accent:* Scrapworks; *Rub-ons:* KI Memories; *Date stamp:* OfficeMax; *Stamping ink:* Stampin' Up! and Clearsnap; *Monogram stamp:* Custom made; *Pen:* Pigment Pro, American Crafts; *Other:* Trim.

142 | YAKITY YAK

DENISE PAULEY

Supplies *Textured cardstock:* DieCuts with a View (red), source unknown (cream); *Patterned papers:* Mustard Moon (text), Creative Imaginations (ABCs); *Fabric:* Junkitz; *Letter stickers:* Sonnets, Creative Imaginations; *Stamping ink:* Fluid Chalk, ColorBox, Clearsnap; *Chalk:* EK Success; *Staples:* Making Memories; *Pen:* Pigma Micron, Sakura.

142 | BASKETBALL 2004-05

ANGIE CRAMER

Supplies *Textured cardstock:* Bazzill Basics Paper; *Letter tiles:* Paper Bliss, Westrim Crafts; *Photo turns:* 7gypsies; *Other:* Brads and word blocks.

143 | ASK YOURSELF

SHELLEY LAMING

Supplies *Textured cardstock:* Bazzill Basics Paper; *Patterned papers:* Anna Griffin and KI Memories; *Flower punch:* Family Treasures; *Pen:* Zig Writer, EK Success; *Other:* Brads.

144 | THROUGH EVERY AGE

SHELLEY LAMING

Supplies *Textured cardstock:* Bazzill Basics Paper; *Printed twill:* Carolee's Creations; *Ribbon:* May Arts (striped), C.M. Offray & Son (heart); *Twist ties:* Pebbles Inc.; *Letter stickers:* Scrapworks; *Stamping ink:* ColorBox, Clearsnap; *Paper flower:* Savvy Stamps; *"Filled with" rubber stamp:* Dawn Houser for Inkadinkado; *Letter stamps:* PSX Design; *Pen:* Zig Writer, EK Success.

144 | PEDICURES AT SUKI

LISA BROWN CAVENEY

Supplies *Patterned papers:* BasicGrey (pink), KI Memories (striped); *Chipboard letters, acrylic paint and rub-ons:* Making Memories; *Pen:* Gelly Roll, Sakura.

145 | ERIN IN SPRING

DENISE PAULEY

Supplies *Textured cardstock:* Bazzill Basics Paper (purple and green), DieCuts with a View (yellow); *Canvas:* K&Company; *Fabric:* Junkitz; *Envelope:* KI Memories; *Letter stamps, hinges and eyelets:* Making Memories; *Stamping ink:* Fresco, Stampa Rosa; *Chalk:* Deluxe Designs; *Sticker:* Art Warehouse, Creative Imaginations; *Tab:* Autumn Leaves; *Pen:* Pigma Micron, Sakura.

146-149 | TRAVEL MINI BOOK

LISA BROWN CAVENEY

Supplies *Patterned papers:* KI Memories, K&Company, Scenic Route Paper Co. and Chatterbox; *Rub-ons:* Making Memories; *Acrylic paint:* Plaid Enterprises; *Pen:* Zig Writer, EK Success; *Other:* Metal chain and chipboard.

150 | M&L

LISA BROWN CAVENEY

Supplies *Patterned paper:* BasicGrey; *Ribbon:* May Arts; *Letter stickers:* American Crafts; *Eyelets:* Making Memories.

150 | HALL OF MIRRORS

LISA BROWN CAVENEY

Supplies *Patterned paper:* K&Company; *Ribbon:* May Arts; *Rub-ons:* Making Memories; *Pen:* Zig Writer, EK Success; *Other:* Mirrors.

151 | MY FAVORITE PLAY

LISA BROWN CAVENEY

Supplies *Patterned paper and ribbon:* KI Memories; *Letter stickers:* Mrs. Grossman's; *Clips:* Barnes & Noble.

151 | DAD & LISA

LISA BROWN CAVENEY

Supplies *Patterned paper:* Scenic Route Paper Co.; *Letter stickers:* me & my BIG ideas; *Ribbon:* Making Memories; *Quote:* Two Peas in a Bucket; *Computer font:* Goudy Old Style, downloaded from the Internet.